Walk with Me

Caring, Living, and Planning Well for Aging Parents

Catherine Fitzhugh

Contents

Foreword	5
Introduction	9
1. Between You and Me	11
2. Family Matters	13
3. Your Spouse and You	21
4. Your Siblings and You	27
5. Your Parents and You	43
6. Miracles and Misfortunes	49
7. Help Me Help You	55
8. Controlling the Finances	63
9. Home Care?	71
10. Manage the Meds	79
11. The Mind Is an Interesting Thing	89
12. You're Not Superman	97
13. Developing Partnerships	103
14. Getting the Bad News	111
15. Come Live with Me	115
16. Assisted Living, Nursing Home, Memory Care	125
17. Dying Well	135
18. Hospice Care	141
19. Celebration of Life	147
20. About the Sorrow	151
21. I Wish I'd Known Then What I Know Now	155
22. Are You Ready?	165
About the Author	167

Copyright © 2022 by Catherine Fitzhugh

Published by Tandem Services Press

Post Office Box 220

Yucaipa, California

www.TandemServicesInk.com

All rights reserved. No part of this book may be reproduced in any form or by any electronic or mechanical means, including information storage and retrieval systems, without written permission from the author, except for the use of brief quotations in a book review.

Ebook ISBN 978-1-954986-13-8

Print ISBN 978-1-954986-12-1

Unless otherwise noted, all Scripture quotations are from the New King James Version®. Copyright © 1982 by Thomas Nelson. Used by permission. All rights reserved.

Scripture quotations marked NIV are from the New International Version. THE HOLY BIBLE, NEW INTERNATIONAL VERSION®, NIV® Copyright © 1973, 1978, 1984, 2011 by Biblica, Inc.® Used by permission. All rights reserved worldwide.

Scripture quotations marked ESV are from the *ESV® Bible (The Holy Bible, English Standard Version®)*, Copyright © 2001 by Crossway, a publishing ministry of Good News Publishers. Used by permission. All rights reserved.

Thanks to Tandem Services for editorial and production services, especially Colleen Tomlinson and Liz Tolsma.

Cover photo credit: Paper and Sage

*To my parents, Verle and Lucile Ackerman,
and Clayton's parents, Jack and Lola Bencek.*

YouTube Video: Life of Dr Verle Ackerman:
https://www.youtube.com/watch?v=UUHym-pv9fE

There's something in my hand to do.
Just another part of life with glorious blessings and sadness.
But the something in my hand is familiar.
It's the hand that nurtured me, guided me, and now needs me.
She said, "You'll *walk with me,*" and I knew where.
The path was uncertain, but the destination was sure.

"Eye has not seen, nor ear heard,
nor have entered into the heart of man,
the things which God has prepared
for those who love Him."
1 Corinthians 2:9

Introduction

I know. You're busy living life. You don't want to think about aging, caring for parents, and especially end-of-life. It's, well—uncomfortable.

If you're like me, you don't like feeling vulnerable, because many of the aspects of care can take you off-guard. And caring well for your loved one can quickly become personal and intense with unfamiliar responsibilities and decisions.

So, let's focus on living well. Whew, that's better. You'll learn how to provide quality care so your parent can live life to the fullest. I'll help you develop a process for planning well, an approach to communicating, and an attitude of confidence.

Make the uncomfortable comfortable. Embrace your personal story by caring well, living well, and planning well.

Chapter 1

Between You and Me

As my dear father slipped into heaven, I was engulfed with familiar pain. My husband and I held each other realizing the finality. No parents. He kissed my forehead. "Well done. Your dad was proud of you." It had been an incredible journey caring for our parents—four contrasts of personalities and physical demands—yet I cherished the path we walked.

At the beginning of care, I'm glad God threw a veil across my future because I wouldn't have felt equipped to navigate the healthcare maze and the barrage of new tasks, not to mention family dynamics, and finally, end-of-life decisions. God's veil allowed me to live in the moment with faith.

So I'm writing this book as me, sitting across the table from you, just talking. It's not a comprehensive text but the story of a family coming together in meaningful ways and the important lessons we learned. Your family will identify with the circumstances and characters in my story—the personalities, financial challenges, time and distance constraints—and realize how each child, sibling, and spouse can provide their unique touch.

The stories answer questions. How do you switch roles with your parents? Can you keep living your life while integrating care? And most important, how do you provide the best quality of life for those you love?

If you're like me, you know your family will be watching and learning. So, your care will be an example for the generation that will care for you. I'll reveal the preparations I wish our parents had made to make it easier so you can rethink your own plans.

Today you may be caring alone or have family support, but know that I've walked this path and offer a lamp for your journey. Regardless of your finances or support, you can plan with confidence and provide meaningful care.

Just So You Know

I never saw myself as a caregiver, the warm and fuzzy type. I didn't know or care to know about hospitals, growing old, or pills. As a kid, I would gag on a tiny allergy pill, and my parents would stand there till I choked it down. I made quite a drama out of it. When an ambulance drove by, I would put my hand over my eyes just in case there was something gross. Caregiver? Not me. But I was a doer. Organized, responsible, I-can-figure-it-out kind of person. Caring? Attentive? Not so much. I seldom shed a tear. But that was then.

Now if you are a caring person, it's a plus. Caring for a loved one will probably be an easier, more logical calling. But for those of us not so inclined, the can-do spirit will get the job done.

Chapter 2

Family Matters

Through the years, family gatherings change unexpectedly—someone will be added, someone will be missing

Family Foundation

The foundation of family relationships, meaning your personal tie with each family member, is established long before the onset of caring. You know every personality, their relationships with each other, and their unique relationship with your parents. Recognizing these nuances is valuable. For example, parents will listen to one child about finances, another child for health advice, or they may depend on one family member for no apparent reason. It can cause strife or be a tool for your parents' cooperation. To hope for change is futile, but using the strengths of the various relationships is a smart strategy.

From the beginning of a parent's declining health to that end-of-life moment will come challenges and emotions that you've never experienced as a family.

Family Dynamics

Clayton and I consider South Florida our home but have also lived in San Francisco and Dallas. Since our children were grown, we've added Detroit and Philadelphia. We love to move and get out of our comfort zone when a new opportunity opens, but it's not for everyone.

I have dear friends that have lived in the same house for forty years. They've had opportunities to move and didn't want to. When I'm with them, I envy their long-term friendships and community roots, but they think our life looks exciting, and it is. Yes, I realize people just don't get us. Most people would be frustrated living our life. In fact, I think I'm finally ready to settle down. Maybe.

Three Children, Three Dynamics

Our adult children have developed their own family dynamics. Even when they lived in the same city, they each led different lives. Not better, just different.

My oldest son, Michael, loves current events and how it relates to Bible prophecy. His world is huge. He reads newsfeeds from every major country every day. I don't relate. But I love his passion, so I engage in endless news analysis. I know more about this scary world than I ever wanted to. But I love my conversations with him. We grow together.

My daughter, Celeste, loves her job and works with the youth at church. In contrast, her world is also huge— an annual passholder at Disney World. I don't share the enthusiasm, and I love my daughter but not enough to stand hours in line for a ninety second ride. Our thing is a weekend at SeaWorld. No lines. Priceless.

My youngest son, Ryan, is a successful realtor. His hobby is exotic fish, and he has a huge aquarium at home. I admit it's beautiful, but he spends money and hours on… fish. I don't get it. But I love him, so I hear about origin, importing, and the care of… fish. It gives us another point of conversation.

However, when the whole family is together, there's not much talk about aquariums, Disney, or world news. Instead,

Clayton and I are entertained listening to our kids' hilarious remember-when-we conversations and about our grandchildren's friends and activities. Even their alfalfa sprouts and smoothies that they consider a 'healthy diet' end up on the dinner table with my pot roast, mashed potatoes, and sweet tea. By the way, Grandparent is the best title I've ever had. Hug 'em, spoil 'em, and give 'em back.

In relation to caregiving, we put no expectations on our children to take a role in our parents' care. They all had an active relationship with their grandparents growing up, usually initiated by our parents. But as they had families and busy schedules, visits were centered around special occasions or holidays.

As the grandparents became less active, each of the children found an activity that was within their comfort level. They would take the grandparents for a ride, sit on the porch, make regular calls, or bring their family. The visits were short, not consistent, but filled everyone's emotional tank till the next time.

Our role was to facilitate special occasions, making sure that our parents had a present to give, with cake and ice cream for everyone. The family fell into a joyful routine with no pressure or judgment.

Meet the Parents: Verle, Lucille, Jack, Lola

Because I will give you intimate insight into the lives of these four people, here are a few sentences of introduction. Throughout the book, you will see the thread of God's hand as their lives unfold.

Verle, my dad, was a minister for over fifty years. He served as a worship leader, then a pastor in South Florida. He saw people's hearts, lifted them up, and took them in. When he walked into a room, he assessed its organization, the spirit of the people, and kept things on schedule. He loved to tease, and people were drawn to him because he was authentic. But his greatest joy was the transformation of lives by teaching and turning hearts to God.

My mom, Lucille, was an educator and accomplished musician. She loved young people and had a keen ability to develop talent. She suffered with poor health, a continual challenge for her and our family. However, she inspired and invested in others and had a deep relationship with God that reflected in every aspect of her life. Dad and Mom were a team and loved their life.

Lola, Clayton's mother, was a stylish, classy lady with an independent spirit and a sharp mind even when she was ninety. She had a career as a business executive in a major department store. She was always in charge, loved her three boys, and cared for people around her.

Clayton's birthfather, Elza, was a perfectionist and meticulous dresser. As a young soldier, he experienced Pearl Harbor and carried the emotional trauma. Elza loved deeply but struggled as an alcoholic. He died when Clayton was twelve. Family life was hard, although more before than after.

Jack, Clayton's stepdad, walked into a ready-made family, brought stability, and changed their lives dramatically. They changed his also.

Our parents had rich and full lives. Holidays were celebrated with wall-to-wall family and friends. They lived large, traveled, had successful careers and loving families. It was often hard to keep track of them. Health didn't get in the way until they were well into retirement, and even then, they spent summers in Maggie Valley, North Carolina, or took long vacations on the west coast of Florida.

But there came the time when their health didn't stay well-in-hand. First, Jack's circulation failed in his leg and resulted in an amputation. It could have been a life changer for them, but they continued living a full life. After Jack was gone, Lola's health began deteriorating. However, she was used to being in charge, and it was a difficult adjustment.

My mom, Lucille, had continual health problems when they retired to the country in North Florida. So they eventually moved near family and friends in Jacksonville. Years later, Dad was diagnosed with Huntington's disease, and the caregiver needed care. All four elderly parents required a wide range of attention.

Family Drama

Every family has some. You know, a problem that needs family support until it comes to pass. That's normal. However, there is drama, and there is DRAMA, the toxic kind. Someone who has frequent conflict never seeing their fault. They are the victim.

But normal family drama, the annoyingly humorous kind, is different from that. It's the big personality that's the center of attention at family gatherings, the mischievous child of oblivious parents, the sudden vegan, the yappy dog that would be so sad left at home, and of course, your politically incorrect uncle. The eye-rolling kind of drama. It's all harmless, but they're yours, so you embrace their weird and smile.

Every occasion builds your family's foundation by offering someone a safe place to share about a new job, a challenging child, marital conflict, a financial crisis, or a health diagnosis. Through the years, your family gatherings will change unexpectedly. Someone will be added, someone will be missing, but today you're making memories.

Family Division and Unity

Years ago, Margaret, my school administrator, said, "You know a mature Christian by the unity they bring." She noticed that unity in the school was always broken by criticism that caused wounds and resulted in people withdrawing. Those divisions in a school or a family can last a long time.

I asked her, "What if someone's going down the wrong path?"

Margaret said, "I don't want any issue to close the door on my influence in their life." Even when they hurt her. She would gracefully let them go but kept the door of friendship open so when they were in need, the relationship was intact for that crucial conversation.

Showing grace is not condoning destructive behavior. In fact, the key to grace is letting consequences play out. Being there but not always available. Allowing space for God to show up is quite a tightrope of wisdom.

A crisis brings out the best and worst in family relationships. Yet it's the time that unity is needed most. Joining minds and hearts is crucial in making right decisions for a parent and for the family. Instead of continuing in criticism or splintering completely, many families lay aside their differences for a short time. They begin to support each other and focus on the meaningful moments together. That short time of unity often blossoms into a new appreciation of their family unit and each other.

Family Heritage

One definition of heritage: Property that descends to an heir, an inheritance. But when I consider my family heritage, it's not monetary. I envision my grandparents' journey through the 1918 Pandemic, the Great Depression, and two World Wars to emerge with strong families of faith. They continued in that faith, making it the cornerstone of their heritage and instilling it in us. Now, in my generation there are eleven cousins with adult children and grandchildren. We all feel the spiritual heritage.

Your family unit of grandparents, parents, uncles, aunts, cousins, brothers, and sisters continues a family heritage. Can you describe your family culture, the heritage? Can you tell the life stories of your grandparents and parents? How they grew up, their relationship with their parents, how they met, their dreams and successes? When they are gone, there's no one left to tell you.

But what if your family heritage has poverty, abuse, or brokenness in its story? Isn't it even more important to know and understand? Those hardships and important lessons of your family story made you who you are, and now, you are the heritage moving forward.

Family Relationships

Are your relationships set up for success? How have you navigated your family cultures, dynamics, and drama? How strong is your family's foundation? There are bumps in the caregiving road ahead because parents aren't always easy, siblings can be hurtful, and children can be insensitive. Resolve to be the one who draws hands together in unity.

Chapter 3

Your Spouse and You

You must enter together, or you will leave apart.

Critical Priorities

How does the conversation begin? Can your marriage end up stronger? How can you add responsibilities without dividing loyalties? Can you prioritize your spouse when time infringements cannot be avoided? What kind of spousal support should you expect?

The truth is, your present relationship with your spouse—communication, conflict resolution, personality, intimacy, and friendship—are indicators of how you will navigate caregiving as a couple. Don't expect your spouse to change who they are; instead, build on who they are. Start by asking what is important to them so your partnership stays the priority.

It Could Happen—Know If It's No

John and Candice made the decision for John's mother to live with them. She was self-sufficient, but dementia caused a demanding demeanor. Candice was an executive assistant and concerned about work and time restraints, but John was self-employed with a flexible schedule and agreed to be responsible for the caregiving. Candice saw the pitfalls but didn't feel like she could say no.

John was good to check on his mom a few times each day, but when Candice came home after work, he was gone, and on the weekends, he played tennis with friends. His mother was often discontented, and Candice was thrown into full-time care when she walked in the door. As John's mother had increasing needs, he realized that he was not equipped and left it all to Candice.

It was obvious that their communication and overall relationship was suffering, and within a year, Candice walked out. John quickly made other arrangements for his mother and worked on their marriage.

Remember, a relationship's problems are often exacerbated by crisis. John should have known that there would be little time for his hobby, and maybe Candice could have provided some weekend caregiving if John had covered the week well. It was obvious to John and Candice that they were not in agreement from the start.

Critical Factors to Discuss

Whose parent is it anyway? If your parent needs care, you want to take the lead in the health decisions. Because your parents are your responsibility, your spouse will normally play a supporting role. But if your spouse is willing to take on the responsibility, first, thank the good Lord. Seriously. Then understand that it will be very important to find that level of responsibility that best supports.

How will that look? Can you get a caregiver, sibling, or friend for a few hours some days so they can have lunch out or do some errands? Perhaps having one day off each week would be better or setting aside time on the weekend for a date.

If your spouse is caregiving all day, take the emotional temperature when you come in the door. Adult conversation is crucial for the caregiver. Hearing and discussing the concerns can be vital, but just as important is talking about other events and people in your lives. A short, quiet conversation makes a huge difference, and those minutes are a lifeline. I don't know how he did it, but Clayton made the conscious effort to leave his exhaustion from the day and uplift us with a few minutes of attention.

Spend one-on-one time with your parent. For you to make informed decisions about your own parent, you will need time alone with them, no matter who is the caregiver. It will give you a gauge of their condition, mentally and physically, and a vital second opinion. A meaningful time with your parent will provide a real look at them and into your spouse's world. It will let your spouse or caregiver know that even though you are tired, the responsibility for your parent is shared.

Let's talk about the issue of gender. It was a lot easier to provide personal care for my mother than my father. It's especially difficult if your wife is caring for her father, or if your husband is caring for his mother. It is a challenge to overcome the intimate personal hygiene barrier, so it may drive decisions about scheduling home care, finding assisted living, or which sibling is best suited to care for a mom or a dad based on gender. Or at some point, you will cross that barrier and find a mutual comfort level.

Finding Harmony—Knowing Who We Are

Like every couple, Clayton and I are very different. How? He is high energy; I savor the journey. He plans for the future; I live in the moment. He can't sit still; I love a comfortable chair. He is impatient; I can endlessly wait. So how have we made such a happy marriage? It's developed. For example, he actually sits to watch sports, so I enjoy sitting with him. I love to discover new places, so our moves have been my adventure. He tries to out-love me, and I let him. I try to out-give him, he lets me. He's an early riser and is very quiet. He falls asleep early, and I enjoy reading. He is tenderhearted; I seldom shed a tear (don't judge). I give more, but I get so much. The point is, we both work at blending our differences. Yes, work.

Today I realize more than ever how we grew as a team. He saw my dad as a great servant of God and wanted to honor him. And even though Clayton loved the corporate world, he also committed to being supportive. Most important, it allowed me to quit my job the last years of their lives and be their full-time caregiver.

Clayton made a point to spend time with them each evening. He put my dad in the car when he went out for an errand or sat and talked about things that mattered to them. Their presence changed our plans, routine, and our life for several years, but we decided together that this was our life. By choice.

What is more important in this world than caring for your spouse, mother, father, or grandparent? It is an honor. Each one of them have sacrificed in their lifetime. In turn, your care will be a vital part of your life story.

Their Example—Our Gift

Clayton and I had great examples of unconditional love between spouses and sacrificial care from grandparents and parents. We didn't wonder how our relationship would look. We witnessed it. We had a blueprint of devotion lived right in front of us. It was an instinctive decision on our part to follow that example and give the same gift to our children. Our family witnessed the devotion between Jack and Lola, Verle and Lucille, just as they witnessed the devotion between their parents.

Elbert and Marie Bowers

My maternal grandfather, Elbert, was a self-taught minister, and Marie loved being a pastor's wife and mother. She was a gentile spirit. He was feisty. They loved country life together in North Florida.

Grandma Marie cooked fresh food from the garden and baked her famous biscuits. Oh, wow. She flattened her homemade dough with a rolling pin and punched out the biscuits with a tin can. We poured dark molasses on our plate and sopped it up with the hot-buttered biscuits.

My memories of them are sweet. Grandpa wasn't always easy, but I observed Grandma's gracious spirit. I also witnessed his attention to the things that were important to her. When I was young, Grandma and I would often watch "The Edge of Night" soap opera. If we heard Grandpa come in, I would get up and click it off because he didn't approve. Then she'd wink, our secret.

In Grandma's final years, after she had a heart attack and stroke, Grandpa completely cared for her. He didn't have money to hire help. He bathed and fed her, cleaned and cooked. We had no idea he could even fry an egg. We admired his example of devotion to her.

At age ninety-six, Grandpa's goal was to read the Bible through one more time. When I visited him, I would pull up a footstool and listen to whatever topic was on his mind. Usually it would be some tidbit from scripture. "Did you know what Samson was afraid of?"

He would squint his eyes and wait for, "No, what?"

Sitting there, I knew I would cherish these sweet moments, and I do.

STERLING AND EDRIS ACKERMAN

My paternal grandfather Sterling and grandmother Edris moved their family from Wisconsin in the '30s to a farm in Georgia, just north of the Florida state line. He was a talented carpenter and could build a delicate clock or a house. He had a work ethic and organization gene that has permeated the Ackerman family for generations. He became an associate pastor in Jacksonville and grew the Sunday school into the thousands with his leadership.

    Edris was a mother of four and a gifted poet but suffered with epilepsy and later Huntington's disease. Grandpa made her care a priority. My dad, Verle, and his sister took responsibility for the household, and it forged a lifelong bond between them. Their self-sufficiency provided life-skills for great achievements, along with the Grandpa Ackerman gene that is still alive and well.

Ancestry Is Mainstream

Today, there's a renewed interest in ancestry among young people. They're researching heritage through their DNA and creating a timeline. The stories of grandparents' relationships and lives die off with each generation unless they are passed on to next generations. Stories of hardships and achievements have great value. It shows more than just what they did. It reveals who they were. Knowing the roots of who we are is the true value of family ancestry.

Chapter 4

Your Siblings and You

Throw away the scale: the weighing of who does the most, who spends the most

A Significant Emotional Event

As siblings, together you will never face a more significant emotional event than your parents' care and end-of-life. You will experience highs and lows with your immediate family, but this event brings your family core back together. Your earliest memories and childhood are wrapped up with your mother, father, sisters, and brothers. It's a family unit that no one else shares.

No matter how you remember your childhood or your parents, their loss will impact you. When you and your siblings are the only ones left, you will see each other in a different light, then if you are the only one left in your family unit, you will feel it.

It's not just a significant event, it's emotional. Several years ago, I attended the viewing of a friend. As I was parking, two grown men in suits were pushing each other against the building, red faced in anger. They were her sons. Later, they were standing in front of her casket with arms around each other. It's emotional.

When my mother was in the hospital, there were siblings in

the next room with their dad. The brother and sister argued and cried in the hall. Decisions had to be made; there had been no planning. The sister was begging, "Don't do this." After the doctor talked with them, hospice came. The brother and sister sat together holding hands. It's significant.

Their dad took care of everything because their mom was frail. He cared for her, paid bills, made appointments, shopped, cooked, and did the housekeeping. When he died in his sleep, the family was in shock. The siblings had always been attentive but so far had little responsibility. It's an event.

The Parent Perspective

Around retirement age, the focus of parents often shifts. A new chapter appears that includes everything from traveling, hobbies, friends, and family to end-of-life planning. If they have insight enough to plan, you are fortunate. And the first thing they analyze is you and your siblings to determine who is capable to do finances, organize daily living, and manage healthcare.

Hopefully your parents have discernment about the dynamics of your sibling relationships. A colleague told my husband, "I have one child who doesn't care about my finances and one who cares too much. One who is sensitive to us, and one who is self-absorbed." Some of your siblings may be trustworthy and cooperative or controlling and difficult, and your parents should understand. After all, they likely had siblings too.

While your parents are pondering this important puzzle, put yourself in their shoes and be a positive, unifying influence in placing each sibling in the most logical spot. The outcome of the puzzle can result in a blessing for everyone or a quagmire for the siblings.

Strategies for Perspective

There's no playbook to navigate caregiving with your siblings, because if you typically haven't worked well together, you still won't work well together, and if you've enjoyed experiences together as adults, you can accomplish good things during this time. So, your lifetime relationship can provide insight into how each sibling will face these challenges now. You'll probably be able to predict their attitudes and actions in most situations.

But just because there's no playbook, doesn't mean there are no strategies. Now's the time to make personal decisions that will help you keep perspective.

Throw Away the Scale

The Scale of Comparison has ruined many sibling relationships because it's never fifty-fifty in any stage of life. It can't be. And deciding who will carry the weight of responsibility often depends on the location and family circumstances of you and your siblings. And yes, to be fair, each sibling should be engaged and contribute whatever they can, but we know that it will seldom be that way. So how will you respond to the imbalance? The weight of this scale hurts the carrier, but ultimately the imbalance of the scale spills on others.

Make the Decision You Can Live With

Jenny chose to throw away the scale when she became the main caregiver for her dad. Her three siblings thought he needed assisted living and began looking for a facility nearby. However, Jenny didn't want her dad to be alone during his last years. He was mentally sharp, but physically unsteady and a fall risk.

She decided for him to live with her family, and he was relieved. His care was wholly on Jenny, and I wondered how she dealt with her siblings' choices. She said, "I wanted a relationship with them, so I let it go. After all it was my decision to care for him, and I'll always be glad I did. We became so close, which made it harder to lose him, but I learned things about him that I would have never known. Those days were priceless to me."

Let It Go

No, I'm not going to break into song. (But you just sang it, didn't you?) It's true, though, you must let some things go because it serves no purpose. We all know that there are some people or circumstances you can't change, no matter what you do. We aren't limiting God; in fact when true change occurs, it will be evident. Let go and let God.

Letting go often involves forgiveness when putting down the scale. I read an article on a friend's blog about forgiveness. "Forgive a Wretch – Like Me?" is the title (lindapue.com). She has wonderful articles that speak to the heart of women. It made me remember that I am so forgiven by God, every day. By his grace he continues to love and forgive me, so I must forgive. God sees me as I am: flawed, selfish, and sinful. Who am I, not to forgive my own brother?

In many cases one sibling carries the load. I did. My brother, my only sibling, was absent. I'll be honest, I had to deal with anger. I picked up and put down that scale a lot. In contrast, I missed him and needed him. But forgiving my brother for his indifference and for the tears my mom shed was the only way I could finally leave the huge scale.

If I carried the weight of bitterness, it would spill over to my parents and steal the joy from our days. When my parents prayed for him at breakfast, my mom cried and couldn't recover, so we all decided to pray for him on our own. The saddest part is that my brother missed the blessing of time with his parents who loved him.

I realized that I couldn't control his decisions, but I could control mine. I decided that if he visited, I would be delighted to see him and not spoil the time for my parents. I would do nothing to make him hesitate to come the next time. I played the scenario over in my head so I would be ready and not blow it. I think it softened me.

One Christmas he was standing at the door. It had been several years. This was not part of the plan, but I burst into tears and stood there hugging him. Mom and Dad added to the bear hug, crying. He didn't know exactly what to do with us, and just said, "Merry Christmas."

It was an awkward day. He spoke little, so we kept the conversation filled with updates on the relatives and the church. He didn't ask how we were and had short answers to our questions about him, but he enjoyed lunch and took a nap in the recliner. When he walked away that day, he knew he was loved. There was nothing else we could do.

I want to say it was because I was so spiritual, but really it was for my parents. My brother's presence was important, and we loved him. So, I wouldn't let my words or actions cause hurt or become an issue. I didn't want to deal with conflict; absence was enough.

In the future, you'll want to remember tender moments with your parents and siblings, not bad feelings. Deep breath, let it go. Could there be a chance, if you let it go, that there will be improvement? At least in you?

The fact remains that there are some decisions that can't be put aside. If you have children, you know that you prioritize and pick your battles. When I had teenagers, I remember thinking, "Is this a hill to die on?" I also tried to think long term. Then you weigh the impact on their immediate life or future happiness. Right now, you are in a similar role of responsibility for your parents, so the strategy is much the same. The tricky part is coming to an agreement with your sibling on serious decisions. What are the strategic factors?

Don't Become the Issue

Respond versus react. This time in your parents' life is too important not to get it right. You're aware of the trigger points for you and your sibling. Do you react or respond? Reacting is actions without thought. Responding is thoughtful words based on your character. Ephesians 4:15 (NIV) says, "Instead, speaking the truth in love, we will grow to become in every respect the mature body..." It's not what you say, it's how you say it, and I'll add, when you say it. In the heat of the moment never reaches the heart and usually wounds.

Carol's brother was an alcoholic. He attended the funeral of their mother, all cleaned up and sober for the occasion. Carol didn't want him there because he was never around when she needed him. She acted out publicly and made a scene.

I spent a few minutes talking with him, and he was apologetic about his life. He slipped out the door quietly. Everyone knew her brother had caused heartache and drama in the family for years, but he looked like the sane one that day and Carol became the issue.

When there's a problem to solve, a hill to die on, standing your ground and speaking your mind may be necessary, but reacting in frustration doesn't bring a better outcome than responding with quiet resolve. A mature response maintains credibility, no matter the outcome.

Be the Adult in the Room

In watching panel discussion or debates, the personalities are usually diverse. There's the jokester, the tough negotiator, the contrarian, and the experienced diplomat. I always say, "Well, there's the adult in the room." No sparring, sarcasm, or name calling, just a summary of everyone's valid points with an experienced perspective. It's an "act like you've been there" analysis.

During this time, there's a lot of noise, personalities, and tasks, so be the adult even if you think no one's listening. It's for your parents; they're getting the benefit of your calm confidence. It's for them.

Keep the Main Thing the Main Thing

The quality care of your parent is the main thing. They are the ones facing aging and end of life. It's personal for them, it's real, and they need physical touch, mental security, emotional peace, and spiritual hope. It's easy to lose sight of their journey ahead.

Conflict and emotions want to take center stage, so learn to buffer yourself and your parents from the fray. The main thing means making every decision link to your parents' care, managing the moving parts, maintaining the calm, and bringing something special into each day.

If your parents are still somewhat independent, you are at the beginning of this journey. Their health needs, your time commitment, and transitioning financial responsibilities will be ever changing for you and your siblings. So, by working as a team, even if it's dysfunctional, you'll walk with them by your side, and you'll be thankful.

Family Culture

Each family has their own culture. Siblings that grow up in the same house, sometimes you'd think they were from different planets. One sibling demands center stage, another is quiet and thoughtful; one sibling finds trouble, the other is responsible. But a bond develops, a history.

When your siblings have their own families, the abilities, beliefs, and personalities within that family unit form a new culture. Criticisms can emerge because you just don't get them despite your history together. In fact, you'll be just as surprised when your own children develop a dynamically different culture for their families.

My friend Kaitlyn's family spent a weekend with her sister, Joy. They grew up in the same house, so how could their lifestyles be so different? Joy and her husband let their children eat whatever whenever and spend endless hours on tech devices with no set bedtime.

Even more puzzling was that Kaitlyn's own children joined their cousins, staying up late, playing video games, eating chips, watching sci-fi movies, and having a blast. Their husbands engaged in laid-back conversations. In fact, everyone had a great time but Kaitlyn.

During our discussion, I learned that her sister's children are straight-A students. In fact, one attends a science/math camp and the other a music camp each summer. They are self-directed, curious, and love learning.

Kaitlyn's family is structured. They emphasize healthy eating, fitness, and organized activities. One child has a rigorous dance schedule, and the other is a star soccer player. It's a busy routine they embrace. Neither culture is right, wrong, or better—just different. Clearly, both families are happy, healthy, and productive.

In fact, their children are a better example of leaning into another culture. They embraced their cousins and loved every minute, and when I made that point to Kaitlyn, she said, "Well, I bet when they come to our house, they won't go outside and play ball."

So? What does it matter? They may play outside, but they all enjoy chips, movies, and video games. "Well, I won't let them eat chips and stay up all night at my house." Why? What harm will a few late nights and a bag of chips do compared to a relationship with their cousins?

The family member that criticizes is usually miserable or the one left out. The rest are having a great time and enjoying each other.

Don't Waste the Season

Just like your family, each of the siblings in our family has their own culture. They don't all see life or live life the same. They sometimes disagree, and like any family, some of the siblings are closer than others. But each of them and their families can fit into the puzzle of caring.

My dad's siblings, Clayton's siblings, and my sibling all had to make individual decisions and contributions. This chapter will show you a variety of ways to participate, but don't think that everyone got along every minute. However, I will tell you that it gave us a new appreciation for each other.

If your sibling is the caregiver, what is your role? If your sibling is being cared for, how can you assist? It's being family. Each sibling can find a special role as parents age. Some responsibilities may be part of a plan, or they may just evolve. For instance, everyone can commit to regular parent calls and updates with your siblings because a variety of viewpoints are valuable. You know, the forest and the trees?

Don't waste the opportunity to support your sibling or have group calls to strengthen your relationships. And remember if the scale is thrown away, the journey will be smoother.

Sibling Power!

Clayton's brother, Fred, lived in Virginia, yet he was diligent about calling Lola. They had a special bond of love. He filled her life with updates about his family and stayed informed about her needs. His family came often to South Florida on vacations, carrying special gifts with them.

Brian lived locally near Lola and Jack. He bore the caregiving load the years that we lived out of state. Brian's initial role was supporting his mother during Jack's decline. He called or checked on them every day and would take Jack out for a walk or to sit by the community pool. At that time, Lola was self-sufficient with Jack, but the daily parent calls were key.

However, when there was an emergency, Brian met them at the emergency room and stayed with them at the hospital. He had a caring spirit, and we were grateful.

Brian always looked for ways to bring joy into their lives. On special occasions, Jack and Lola would celebrate with Brian's family, but if they didn't feel up to it, he would show up with a grocery sack of food at noon and cook steaks and baked potatoes. He would have festive plates and napkins and set up a picnic on their porch. Then he would go and do the same for his family.

After Jack died, Lola's health began declining. Brian's role increased considerably. Lola wanted to be at home as long as she could, so Brian coordinated her home care, drove her to doctor's appointments and physical therapy. It was difficult as a son to provide personal care for his mother, so he was dependent on caregivers. When Lola could no longer be alone, Brian was attentive through her time in a nursing home. Again, the calls from family and the frequent visits were her main source of joy.

How did we support Brian during those years? When we lived out of state, Clayton flew to see his parents, and we both were there for Christmas and dedicated our vacations to family. Seeing Lola and Jack often helped us understand what Brian was facing and how we could help. We were fortunate to live in South Florida for the last years of Jack's life. During that time, we were able to offer more tangible support, but Brian was always the faithful caregiver to them, an example to his children, and a blessing to us.

Verle's Siblings

My dad's siblings, two brothers and a sister, each found their role in his life. They stepped in with touches from God himself. I still get emotional when I think of their sacrifice.

Bill was ten years younger than my dad. When my parents moved to Jacksonville, they were near Uncle Bill and Aunt Delores. Bill and my dad were close, and he loved my sweet mom. He had a daily routine—walked in the front door, went directly to the cookie jar, kissed Lucille on the forehead, and sat in the recliner. The three of them would chat, then he and Dad would run an errand or set another place at the table for lunch.

When my dad couldn't drive anymore, Bill took over all the errands and transportation. Bill drove them to church, took them to Cracker Barrel, ran errands for them, and bought groceries. It became a big responsibility, but he stepped up without hesitation. I never even asked him to help. He just loved his brother.

Aunt Delores was still working at home as a medical transcriber, but she included my parents for special occasions. They both thought of ways to bring joy into my parents' life.

Later, when my parents lived with me, Uncle Bill would come and stay with them so Clayton and I could take a vacation. What a gift for us. How do you say thank you to family members that sacrifice and care that way? It leaves me speechless.

Russ and His Clan

Russ was twenty years younger than my father. He was born when my dad was in college. Their bond is amazing even though they never lived in the same house. Russ and Judy were still working, but they visited and took them out to eat. They have three grown children and a slew of grandchildren. They all move as one unit. No kidding. When Russ and Judy plan something, everyone shows up, along with a few stragglers. Everyone brings mounds of food and there's a celebration for something. Anything.

My parents loved Christmas and always decorated every corner of the house, inside and out. Dad had to buy a shed for the decorations. One year he realized that he was getting too insecure to climb a ladder and could no longer decorate.

So on the Saturday after Thanksgiving, a caravan of elves pulled in front of my parents' house. Out poured Russ and Judy's clan—my cousins, their wives, the children, babies, and platters of food. The children surprised my parents by yelling, "Merry Christmas!"

When the door opened, the children burst in to decorate the house. By that time, all the guys were bringing the decorations onto the porch. Mom was in her glory, directing where to put the tree and where to hang the wreaths, stockings, and lighted garland. I can still see her face with all the little ones crowded around, talking at once. The guys took over the outside as Dad watched from the porch. At the end of the evening, the tree was glistening inside, and the house was festive outside. An annual tradition had begun.

Years later, my parents moved to Pennsylvania to live with us. One Thanksgiving, Russ and Judy's whole clan drove twelve hours in a caravan to surprise my parents. My mom and dad answered the door and again the children yelled, "Surprise!" It was a blessed time together as they again decorated for Christmas. It was a Thanksgiving we will always cherish because in less than a month we were all gathered in Jacksonville for my mom's funeral. You just never know.

Joanne—Dad's Sister and Encourager

Joanne is five years younger than my dad and is the only girl in the family. Joanne can do anything she puts her mind to. She was an educator and pastor's wife. She also quilts and plays the piano. Aunt Joanne and Dad called each other regularly and carried each other in their hearts.

Because they were the two oldest children, they had much of the household responsibility growing up because of their mother's illness. Joanne and Dad learned to cook, clean, wash, sew, and care for Bill and Russ. So early in life, they became capable and responsible. Their hardship bonded them and made them strong.

When my dad was diagnosed with Huntington's disease at eighty, it devastated Joanne because the family had watched their mother suffer and die with the disease. Huntington's is hereditary, and the diagnosis changed everything for Dad and me and shocked his siblings. Usually the disease begins at forty, so we assumed that no siblings had carried the gene from their mother. Not so.

Aunt Joanne stepped into my life right away. She not only wanted to monitor how Dad was doing, but she wanted to encourage me. My mom was still alive but very childlike. Aunt Joanne seemed to sense what I needed and would send a text saying that she loved me and was praying for me. Occasionally I had a day that I struggled, and she was on the phone.

As my dad declined, she made visits to see him. They would look over all the photo albums of their family, and she would try to help him remember stories about the days growing up. They would sing hymns together. She and I had long talks about their childhood, and I learned to appreciate and love her and my dad even more.

Toward the end, Dad still knew her voice. She would call and say, "Verle, do you know who this is?"

In his frail voice, he would answer, "My sweet, sweet sister."

My Younger Brother, Rick

In the early days of writing this book, I didn't know how to discuss Rick. I wanted to write this book with care and be gracious to him and others. But my brother's story took one of those unexpected turns into a family's testimony of sorrow and grace. So in the telling, know the intent of my heart is love.

Rick received a lion's share of musical talent. He created and directed musical productions in churches during Christmas and

Easter that rivaled Disney or Broadway. It included a hundred-voice choir, drama, and a forty-piece orchestra complete with professional sets of his creation. Thousands of people attended the performances over the holidays.

Rick, his wife, and I sang together, and our families enjoyed a close relationship. We were fortunate to live near our parents many of those years, and even though Rick was younger, I looked up to him and counted on him as my dear brother.

Many of you have had a loved one lose their way. Whether it's drinking, drugs, wrong relationships, or just a series of bad choices, they become lost to us. It's heartbreaking. No matter what you do, nothing helps. This was Rick. He walked away from a thirty-year marriage and two adult sons over fifteen years ago, only showing up occasionally. His parents, sibling, spouse, children, grandchildren lost the relationship. There's always more to the story, but respectfully, I'll not go into more detail.

During the decline of my parents, we all struggled, missing him. Mom had dementia and didn't understand why Rick wasn't there, and Dad worried about him. I sure could have used my brother. I didn't need him to do anything, just care. He came to my parents' house for Christmas a few times. I spent time with him, so he knew I loved him and always had a present for him, just in case.

When Mom and Dad were close to dying, I left voice messages and emails. His sons talked with him, but he was not able to come to the funerals. He was not my brother, the one I knew, but I missed him.

In 2020 during the time of COVID-19, Rick was diagnosed with cancer and kidney failure. His sons informed me, so I called his hospital room. No one was allowed to visit. He was so sick and disoriented, but over the next months, we talked every day on the phone. His medication eased his discomfort, and we both found our sweet relationship again. I never brought up the past—just was his sister, caring about him. I spent time talking with the nurses and doctors and got regular updates. They had to give him the hard news, and we spent time talking about his wishes.

His adult sons, Rusty and Richy, had been talking to him daily. Richy lives in Texas, and Rusty lives several hours away from the hospital. End of life discussions were difficult to hear, but the doctor recommended home hospice and talked about discharging him. Rick was going home alone in poor living conditions.

Rusty and Richy called me to discuss next steps. At this point, I had no expectations or condemnation of any decisions they would make concerning his care. There were wounds with his sons and no connection with his teenage grandchildren. But over the years, Rusty and Richy had always treated their dad with respect and attempted to help.

Rusty's wife and family opened their hearts and home to Rick. They picked him up from the hospital the next morning and brought him back home. Richy and his family drove from Texas. Over the next few weeks, Rick was surrounded by family including grandchildren. They loved and cared for him as he slipped into deep rest and then heaven.

The ending could have been so different, but the grace that was shown by his boys was a testimony to their relationship with God. I was overwhelmed by them and so grateful for their tender care. God is sovereign for allowing my brother and I to mend. Praise the Lord for His mercies. God not only provided love for my brother, but He touched Rusty, Richy, and me.

Chapter 5

Your Parents and You

Roles begin, separate, then meet again

Life's Roles and Phases

For decades parents raise a family who are dependent on them. Then, children embrace parenthood and parents transition to grandparents. Children, parents, grandparents—all interdependent. Roles and phases that weave together, separate, then meet again.

Your parents walk with you through childhood, yet childhood was your own experience. You'll walk with your parents through end-of-life, but it will be their own experience. That final shared experience is the encore of a life-long relationship.

Then There Was One

Under most circumstances, you will only have to care for one parent. Usually Mom will care for Dad, then she is left alone or the other way around. So it's unusual for both parents to need care at the same time like mine did.

Clayton and I talk about being the one left, and neither of us want to face life alone, but one of us will. One of us won't get their care. I know how hard it is to lose a parent, but losing a spouse shakes every thread of your life and blurs the future. There is the uncertainty of who will be there with you and how to navigate life alone. So be aware that your last parent will require a deeper understanding.

It's helpful to remember the phase of life that weaved them together and the devotion that grew from trials and triumphs of their life well-loved. The Hollywood love that we spend endless hours watching is a phony imitation of what I witnessed during our parents' final years together. It was a result of their compelling love story.

Jack and Lola's Love Story

When Jack met Lola, he was alone in the world, no children or siblings. He didn't speak fondly about his childhood. And as a young man in the military, he faced heartbreak as he cared for his wife with terminal cancer. Many years later, Jack still didn't feel like he belonged to anyone, anywhere.

But then he met Lola, a lady with style and confidence, who was also longing for love. Opposites—gruff and grace—attracted and filled the emptiness. He offered stability and security; she offered a place to belong.

When Jack came into their lives, Lola had three sons: Fred, Clayton, and Brian. Her oldest, Fred, was grown, but her two younger boys, Clayton and Brian, ages eleven and ten, were still at home. Initially Jack was tough but slowly allowed himself to be accepted by his ready-made family. Lola, Clayton, and Brian were thankful for a safe and stable environment, and eventually Jack's gruffness turned to kindness. He was truly loved and called Dad. Over the years, the grandchildren softened him even more, and he learned to open his heart. Whatever wounds that made him put up a wall were healed.

Jack was not a religious man, but he knew that Clayton and Brian's families had a strong faith. When we would all gather for a meal at Jack and Lola's house, we would join hands and say a prayer. He would sit at the end of the table with his hands in his lap and his eyes wide open. He didn't want anything to do with it.

One morning Clayton and Jack were sitting on the porch. The subject of death and heaven came up. Clayton shared his faith, and Jack indicated that he had been considering God. Clayton said, "I don't want to be in heaven without you, Dad."

Jack prayed with faith that day to give his life to God. It was a sweet, sincere decision. When the family gathered for supper, we were surprised that Jack was the first to reach out his hands and bow his head for prayer. We could hardly pray for the shock of it. We realized that it had taken years of a family's love for Jack to accept God's love.

Years later, Lola took care of Jack as he declined physically and mentally, including a leg amputation. They both had been heavy smokers, and when the circulation to Jack's leg failed, he had the surgery. His dementia was also changing his personality, and he was easily agitated, suspicious, and became hard to control. Lola pushed him in his wheelchair up and down ramps, put the chair into the car, and managed to bathe and clothe him. She was small and mighty at 115 pounds, but it took a toll on her.

I watched as she tenderly cared for him. She wouldn't even discuss a nursing home for her Jack. He had come into her life, helped her raise her boys, and changed their lives significantly. They had lived a full and happy life together, and this was part of it.

Their long-time doctor intervened and had a crucial conversation with Lola about a nursing facility for Jack. It was a good decision because his mental and physical challenges were beyond what one person could handle. So Lola sat by his side every morning and afternoon for a year before he went to heaven. She was determined to give him the devotion he had given her all those years, and we watched the sacrificial love of Lola for her Jack.

It was enriching for us and our children to witness a clear example of how to carry ourselves with grace. She didn't make it seem a hardship, just another part of their life.

Verle and Lucille's Love Story

My parents, Verle and Lucille, were engaged at nineteen. As a young man, Verle had the attention of the executives at Independent Life Insurance in downtown Jacksonville. They told him he had a bright career ahead of him, so their plans were built around that career. Verle was taking night classes while working full time. Lucille had just completed high school and was planning for their wedding.

One Friday night, their church had a special speaker from a seminary in Fort Worth. Lucille went to the service with friends while Verle was attending night school. The speaker spoke passionately about the seminary and a life of ministry. Lucille had grown up in a minister's family and always had a heart for God. She felt the Lord speaking to her about seminary and developing her music skills, but she also knew that leaving would end her future with Verle. During that service, Lucille made the decision to go to seminary.

Verle's classes were dismissed early that night, and he slipped into the back of the church. His heart was also moved. He envisioned himself as a music minister and giving his life to God for ministry. He knew, though, that leaving would end his future with Lucille, and during the service he also made the decision to go. Lucille didn't even know Verle was in the building.

After the service, they realized that they had simultaneously made the same decision. They were married two months later and left for seminary. It was the beginning of a great team. Lucille mastered the piano and organ, and Verle developed his music and business skills.

The two of them performed and conducted great musicals and developed the talents of musicians for over fifty years. All their music centered around their love for the Lord and their heart for people. Lucille trained musical groups and played the organ and piano while Verle conducted the choir and congregation as music minister.

Despite Lucille's health challenges, she lived life to the fullest as an educator and musician. They both worked full time—Verle at the church and Lucille at a Christian school. After twenty-five years as a music minister, Verle became a pastor. The church grew from 500 to 2,500, along with a Christian school of 1,500 students. They loved working side by side in ministry, and their heart for people impacted thousands.

During retirement, Verle was a full-time caregiver to Lucille. He always said, "Lucille needs this. Your mama wants that. I'm doing this for her." He had learned to cook at an early age and had also cooked at youth camps for years. He was a jack-of-all-trades, and it came in handy in Lucille's care as he approached each day with reckless abandon. He had been pastor to thousands, then became caregiver to one.

Roles and Phases Meet Again

Even when your roles switch, you are still a son or daughter. The new phase begins as a helping hand that enables your parents to care for each other and maintain a full life. Then, when there is one, you'll attempt to fill the void of care that would have been. You pick up that final phase for the spouse that's gone.

Jack loved trips, so Clayton's brother, Brian, would take them on day trips. Lola wanted to make sure her finances were done properly. Credit score still mattered. After Jack was gone, she told me that she missed a human touch—someone's hand to hold, a hug, or a kiss. So, I became purposeful in wrapping her in my arms and or walking hand in hand.

My parents loved Cracker Barrel, and that became our weekly lunch out. When Mom was gone, my dad missed buying things for her. "If your mom was here, I'd get that for her."

"I like that too, Dad!"

It gave him joy when he found something I needed. Out would come the credit card.

I wasn't part of their love story, but I was part of their life story.

Chapter 6

Miracles and Misfortunes

A medical mindset

The Suwannee River ran through the small town of Branford, Florida, where my parents retired. Their house sat opposite my grandparent's house on four acres that had been in our family since I was a child. The dark-brown house had a deep front porch with six white rocking chairs and beautiful fern baskets hanging from the eave. The perch from those rockers had live entertainment from birds and squirrels taunting each other, or a quiet family of deer. It was a park setting complete with picnic tables under the pines and benches surrounding a roaring firepit.

A wood fence stretched around the perimeter with swinging gates that Dad opened each morning to retrieve the paper. Tire ruts created a long, shaded drive that softly curved around the towering trees. Pinecones and leaves crunched as a car meandered its way toward the house.

It was such a peaceful, quiet place. I would take a deep breath as I drove in, remembering many joyous Thanksgivings. Our extended family would arrive and crowd the tables with farm-fresh food. Flour would splatter aprons. There were potholders, colorful dishes, pitchers of sweet tea. In the evening, while the adults sat around a bonfire, the kids made use of the open acres playing hide and seek, just happy to be together.

Medicine Misfortunes

A few weeks before Thanksgiving, Dad called me. It was their first year of retirement. Mom was not communicating and had become disoriented. She wouldn't even respond on the phone. So my family decided to arrive early Thanksgiving week.

Mom was hardly aware of us and what was going on around her. When I pushed her to engage, she would stare at me with her little blue eyes like she knew something was wrong. I kept her close and had her ride with me into town on an errand. When we pulled back down the drive, she blurted out, "Cathy, where am I? Is this home?"

I was a bit startled and asked if she recognized it.

She said, "I'm afraid." Those were the only few words she had said for days.

Her Jacksonville doctors, several hours away, were unavailable, so Dad made an emergency appointment with the local doctor for the next day. He asked that we bring her medications, and I was shocked by the number of prescriptions. The next day this young, country doctor took her vitals, looked at her medications, and asked questions about her health history.

Two of her health problems had been migraines and diabetes, but her primary diagnosis was a neuropathy disease that burned away her right hand and arm muscles. It was discovered at Mayo Clinic, but no one knew the specific name, cause, or treatment. Mom was an organist and pianist before this painful disease began years earlier, and now her right hand and arm hung limp by her side.

The new doctor immediately believed that some of the medication was the cause of the disorientation, so over a few weeks he pared back the number of medications to four. His approach was right, because one evening I received a call and heard my mom's voice say, "Hello sweet daughter!"

That morning she had started talking up a storm. She was back. Dad and I were relieved. Over the next few days, she said she didn't remember Thanksgiving but knew something was wrong.

I have to say that the wisdom of that small-town doctor provided my first lesson about medication and physicians. It changed my approach to caregiving for the next thirty years.

The lesson was obvious. When someone feels sick or has unusual behavior, check their medications first. Every single time. I say it enough that my family says it for me. Check the meds first. Don't automatically assume that confusion, mental decline, or feeling bad is just old age or an illness. If you get nothing else from this entire book, please learn the simple steps to manage medications, including vitamins. It's not just for the elderly, it's for each of us, including our children and our families.

My mother-in-law, Lola, had been feeling queasy every morning for months. She lost her appetite, dropped weight, and was too tired to get up. She was declining quickly. I knew to check her medications and discovered that she had started a cholesterol pill earlier that month. She decided to skip it a few days. It took less than a day. In fact, the first morning the nausea disappeared, and she began eating that day. She talked to her doctor and made the decision to make diet adjustments and choose quality of life. She had a full recovery.

My husband, Clayton, had ringing in his ears for several weeks. He had just started a medication, and when he discontinued it, the ringing went away within a few days. Ringing in the ears was not a common side effect of that medication, but it was in the list of seldom or rare side effects. Anyway, we followed the process, and it worked. The doctor had wanted to treat the ringing in his ears with another medication to treat the side effect of the first medication.

A young man, Dave, was given a prescription for neuropathy pain in his legs and feet. It wasn't a pain pill, so he agreed to give it a try. After a few weeks, he became depressed and shared with his wife that he had been having thoughts of suicide. She immediately looked at the prescription information and found that depression and thoughts of suicide were a common side effect. He lowered the dosage to one pill per day, the depression lifted, and it was enough to ease the pain.

What could have been the results? Most people would have considered Lola's weakness a sign of old age and allowed her to deteriorate when she had healthy years left. Clayton would have received an additional medication for the ringing in his ears, and Dave would have been given an antidepressant and counseling. All three would have had complications instead of recovery.

Medicine Miracles

My mom, Lucille, had migraine headaches since she was fourteen. Over the years, there were treatments developed other than icepacks or a pain injection at the emergency room, but they weren't always effective. On one trip to the ER, her blood pressure was slightly elevated, and the attending physician gave her a blood pressure prescription.

About three months later, my dad mentioned that Mom had not had a migraine in a long time. I asked him if she was on any new meds, and he gave me the name of the blood pressure medication. Believe it or not, that medication had been shown to prevent migraines in some people. She was sixty-one and had had migraines once or twice a month since she was fourteen. She never had another migraine. Never. Needless to say, even though she did not have high blood pressure, she took that tiny pill the rest of her life. By the way, there are other medications that have a side effect that prevents migraines in some people.

As we watched my mom's neuropathy disease progress in her arm, her pain management became more of a challenge. She always carried ice packs in her purse to take the edge off the pain in her arm and shoulder.

One Christmas, she fell and broke her pelvis. After the surgery, she was in rehab for several weeks. As usual, some days were good pain days, and other days were bad pain days. But because of the disease, there was always pain. Anyway, I knew her routine. She would begin asking how much longer until her medication about thirty minutes before medication rounds.

However, the second week in the rehab, I asked her what her pain level was, and she said, "Okay." That never happened. So I quickly went to the nurses' station and saw a new medication on her list, Cymbalta. I looked it up and realized that it was not a drug but a medication to treat neuropathy nerve pain.

Her primary care doctor said the surgeon had prescribed it. We agreed to slowly reduce the pain medication for her neuropathy, and within a week, the medication was less than half. She had good pain days and sometimes better than that. The pain relief changed her whole spirit and impacted the dynamic of care. It was another real medicine miracle.

You may have your own misfortune and miracle stories. I hope that these will create a new mindset that will help you manage not only the medications but the physicians. Why both? Because they go hand in hand. Think about this: When a medication is prescribed by your doctors, they don't see you again for weeks or maybe months. Whose care are you under during that time? You. You become the health manager twenty-four/seven.

Chapter 7

Help Me Help You

Sometimes you can't save people from themselves

It's an uncomfortable transition, parent and child changing roles. It often feels disrespectful to take control, to make decisions, especially when your parent is defensive about yielding control. But this is a battle that can't be won, because neither wins if there's a loser. We know it's difficult to change after seventy years or more, especially when you lose control of your own life decisions.

It's equally difficult if your parent is mentally sharp but not sharp enough. Their pride or stubbornness can lead to a decision that impacts their future comfort. They don't want to be a burden, but they need you to be there. They won't cooperate, and you finally must let them make their own decisions. Parent and child changing roles. You think, "If they do this, they'll live to regret it." Hmm. Where did you hear that before? Strange, isn't it?

Sometimes There Is No Answer

This week my friend, Pamela, age fifty-five, is so frustrated with her eighty-five-year-old parents, that she's walking away and giving up. They have been in poor health and have mismanaged their finances for years. Her brother has helped physically, financially, and even offered for the parents to live with him, but they won't leave their home.

Pamela still works fulltime but moved in to assist with their care and contribute some financial relief. Their bills far exceed their income, and they continue to run up debt. All suggestions to downsize and create a manageable life were denied. Pamela caught up some of their overdue bills, but they are financially upside-down and refuse to let her handle the budget. They cannot physically live alone, but she is moving out, brokenhearted and frustrated. The whole family is just wondering what's next.

A Systematic Transition

I remember driving my daughter to LSU her first year. We had a six-hour drive, and I felt compelled to summarize eighteen years of parenting in six hours! I doubt if it changed the course of, well, anything. In fact, it blurred as soon as we saw Mike the Tiger's cage in the middle of campus. Driving back home, I had to laugh at myself, knowing that lessons are learned through systematic conversations and hands-on experiences.

Just as we realize the empty-nest transition can't be ignored, neither can the transition of aging. So it's better to have everything planned, no waiting till the drive. By their seventies, parents should begin a discussion about their wishes and care options. If your parents don't seem to have a plan, the family can begin to ask their thoughts about the future. Assure them that it's not about money but knowing how you can help them. "Help me help you" starts now.

The tough stuff—their funeral arrangements, financial plan, important files, and each child understanding their role—creates a foundation for transition. Notice I didn't say flawless or easy. By the time my parents were unable to care for themselves, I knew the bills, ordering the medication, and coordinating care

—first discussing, then watching, then doing. What a gift for us! Chapters eight and twenty-one discuss planning and transitioning.

Early Crucial Conversations

Get ready for some crucial conversations. The keys to the car, finances, moving, home care, assisted living, end-of-life philosophies. Talk about these scenarios. Discuss this book or the families around you that are walking through these decisions right now. Know your parents' thoughts and promote discussions. Refer to chapter twenty-one in this book.

When it comes to care, some parents, siblings, or spouses will be reasonable and cooperative, but others will be stubborn and independent. It makes caring not only difficult but often miserable for everyone. What if they refuse to see a doctor, allow for home care, or continue to drive? Sometimes you can't do anything for them. Consequences are of their own doing.

My Sacrifice Is to Care for You. Your Sacrifice Is to Make It Easy for Me.

When my parents first retired in their mid-sixties and lived on the property with my grandparents, they knew that the grandparents needed attention. My mom loved living out in the country, and literally, the chickens from the farm next door woke them up each morning. Mom loved the trees, deer, birds, and squirrels. You get the picture. After my grandfather died, Mom's health was deteriorating, and my parents needed to be near Dad's family in Jacksonville.

The week Dad and I cleaned the fence row around the perimeter of the property, I realized that four acres were just too hard for him to maintain. All the weeds and bushes had grown into the fence and had to be removed by hand. It felt like a hundred acres, and I admit that Dad did much better than I did.

However, I saw that he was weary of the outside work along with all the cooking, cleaning, and caring. For the first time, I realized that he was slowing down.

They really needed to sell this home in the country that had been in the family for over fifty years, but Mom was not having it. She never wanted to leave this place, and I could see the disappointment in her eyes. She wasn't thrilled with moving to a neighborhood with people instead of chickens. She wanted trees and deer in the backyard.

No one knew the sacrifice ahead for all of us, but right now it required a big sacrifice from her. And it was one of the first times we reversed roles. She wasn't always clear of mind, but a heart-to-heart was necessary. So I approached it this way.

"This move isn't just about our wants, Mom. It's about Dad too. You can see that he is weary and is aging. It's time for us to do what is best for him this time. You don't want to find him sick one day and wish we had done things differently. He has been there for all of us our whole lives, and now we need to begin caring for him."

Well, it worked. Mom stood up and said, "Where are the boxes?" God bless her.

Every time I think about that move—fifty years of stuff—it makes me laugh. Mom hovered over Dad and me because she didn't want anything thrown away. I always try to avoid a fight with my mama. So, we encouraged long naps, and while she slept, we slipped things into the truck. Dad and I drove at least ten truckloads of junk to the dump. This is one of the times I took advantage of Mom's forgetful little mind. Sneaky, huh?

I never heard another word of dissent from Mom through the whole move, but the day we pulled away from the house, I realized the real emotional connection to the house. She looked back and said, "Bye, Momma. Bye, Daddy," even though they had been in heaven for years. Her memories of them were still there.

Clayton and Dad searched for the perfect house for Mom in

Jacksonville. It backed up to a nature preserve with trees, and a family of deer were often in the backyard. The move to Jacksonville allowed them seven more years of independence. Their church was attentive by visiting and bringing food. Dad's family of brothers, sisters-in-law, nieces, and nephews all honored and loved them.

You Can't Save People from Themselves

Lola, Clayton's mom, knows what she wants, and those of us who are family, know that it's her way or the highway. It was her only way of surviving when she grew up. Her mom and dad divorced when she was young, and her brother chose to live with their wealthy father. Lola knew she couldn't leave her mom alone. It was a clear case of the haves and the have-nots, and Lola was forced to hold her head up and achieve on her own. She was shamed by the rest of her family because she stayed with her mom.

Her father gave her brother a car, an education, and the prestige that went with it. He became a lawyer, then a judge, but Lola had to work hard and make her own breaks. She climbed the ladder in the retail business and became the highest paid female in the corporation. She was highly respected and loved by her employees and colleagues.

She had suffered bad marriages, which included Clayton and Brian's father who was an alcoholic. It had been a tough stretch of years before she married Jack. Through it all, she maintained her confidence and determination. Her way or the highway was the only way she knew. She was fiercely loyal and took care of everyone around her.

Lola loved her three boys, and luckily, she loved me too. We were joined at the heart from the beginning. If I made her Clayton happy, I was in. We spent quite a lot of time together over the years, and she called me Prissy.

It was hard watching her become frail and insecure after Jack died. I always told her that she could come live with us when she couldn't live alone and I would take care of her. But she wanted to be home. We arranged for home care, but she thought it was a waste of money. She constantly told them to leave, but as soon as they were gone, she complained that no one came to see her.

At night she double bolted the front door and was frightened all night. Her friends and neighbors would corner us and tell us to do something because she shouldn't be alone. We agreed. But short of throwing her over our shoulder and taking her out kicking and screaming, what could we do?

One time after a surgery, we lived nearby, so I brought her home with me to recover. We sat on the back porch together, and I made her fresh snacks in the afternoon. I waited on her hand and foot.

Clayton came home one evening and said, "How was your day?"

She said, "Not very good. I want to go home." So that was it. She could make her own choices. But I believe she didn't want to interfere in our lives, and her stubbornness was a way of protecting us.

A few years later, she was hospitalized, and the doctor arranged a skilled nursing facility. Luckily she agreed to stay there and be cared for. However, she didn't watch television, wouldn't eat in the dining room with the "old people," and refused to go to physical therapy. I had to go against my better judgment and let her have it her way. Clayton and I still had many sweet moments with her, and again, Brian was on constant watch when we were long distance. He blessed us all.

Lola went to heaven exactly two months after my mom. Many days during that last year, I would call Lola, and she would be too weak or confused, and we wouldn't have much of a conversation. But the day my mom died, she was my first call. She answered and I said, "Hi, it's me. I needed to call you. My mom just died, and I wanted to hear your voice."

We were both blessed that she had a rare moment of clarity.

She told me how good God was to give me such a sweet mother and what a wonderful daughter I had been to my mom. She told me that I would be all right, but it would take time. She thanked me for loving her boy and making him happy and that she loved me more than I knew. I told her I loved her too. She said, "Goodbye, Prissy." I didn't know it then, but that was our last conversation.

    Lesson: Sometimes you can only do so much. People may make decisions that impact them negatively, but you continue to hold them close and love them through their own choices.

Chapter 8

Controlling the Finances

The Issue of Trust

"You took my money! Where is it?" Jack's angry words were coming from the laundry room. Dollar bills were stuck to the drum of the washer. I stood behind him holding a second load. Guilty of doing the wash. The first load had obviously exposed the First National Pillowcase Bank.

In Jack's later years, he imagined people taking his money, so Lola played along. She supplied dollar bills to pacify him, and he hid them. She would find his hiding place, which he forgot about, and give the bills back to him. The exercise made him feel in control, except I accidently laundered his money. He was suspicious of me after that.

Financial responsibility can be the result of a sudden health event or a gradual process from parent to child. Trust can feel like a barrier, but a parent's reluctance is not about trust in you but fear of losing control, losing peace of mind, running out of money, of not knowing. It's a desperate fear. It's real. So how can you move forward, helping them maintain peace of mind about their life, their future, their financial security? That's really it, isn't it?

Let's be honest. Handing over the finances is much easier when the child is trustworthy and has shown financial capability as an adult. Think about your personal security. What if you had to give someone every financial account, credit card, and bill to manage for the rest of your life? I imagine you would prefer a gradual timeframe to teach them, watch them, then at least receive reports. That sounds respectful and reasonable, a logical step-by-step transition.

First, watch and learn. Then gradually transition, and finally take control and report.

IN THE BEST-CASE SCENARIO, the watch and learn step occurs years before with occasional updates, then you ease into the gradual transition phase over time. Depending on physical or mental challenges, the take control part can transition naturally or suddenly. But this discussion about their plans is a wise decision as parents approach retirement because it never really occurs by anyone's plan. The only sure thing? It will occur. You will have to unravel it on your own at the end, or you will be prepared ahead of time

At Least It's Not Chickens

In the 1930s and '40s, when my grandfather Bowers was a young man, he pastored three country churches at the same time in North Florida. He applied for the first church-bus tag for the state of Florida and drove it down dirt roads every Sunday, picking up waiting families. He would preach on Sunday morning at one church, then drive to another church for the evening service, then another on Wednesday night. This shiny bus was a novelty, and when children rode alone, my Grandma Marie took responsibility for them along with her own little girl, Lucille. Everyone was everyone's business.

People don't believe this, but my grandfather was actually

paid in live chickens, baskets of vegetables, eggs, and a few dollars thrown in. It was a different world then. Thank goodness. Grandpa had a job at the pharmacy during the week in addition to cultivating large gardens at home. His open Bible sat on the pharmacy counter as he pondered his Sunday message and jotted notes in the margins.

The town knew that Grandma Marie always had a pot of stew and hot biscuits for the hungry. The regulars, along with several strangers, found her kitchen screen door and called for Marie. They waited at a small picnic table nestled between two shade trees or sat on the back steps. She fed their bodies and souls.

During the depression, those country churches became a place of solace for hundreds of families, then after the war, the Bowers moved to South Florida and established a flourishing church that he pastored for almost twenty years. Grandpa Bowers and Marie then retired back on the property in North Florida.

That same acreage seemed like an idyllic place for my parents, Verle and Lucille, to retire with my grandparents. Dad was still sharp, healthy, and worked part time at a local church. Even during retirement, he put his pastor's hat back on, listening intently to young pastors and encouraging them in their ministry.

I often wondered what Dad was thinking in his heart, having left a thriving ministry just months before, and now his primary responsibility was to care for a large property and everyone on it—cooking, cleaning, mowing, then driving a small pickup to shop in a one-street town, stopping by the local dumpster to toss in the trash. But he did it with the same enthusiasm as standing before thousands and had the same tenderness as when praying with a family. It was still his calling, ministering to three of God's precious saints.

My dad had his home office organized with all the bills and files in meticulous order. He had a picture of his church on the wall with over a thousand members gathered outside. He is standing in front of them with a bullhorn. It always makes me smile when I remember that day because several Sundays before, he was having fun with the congregation and said that he would sing "America" in the middle of highway 441 if there were over 2,000 in attendance on July Fourth weekend.

Well, there were, and everyone held him to it. He had to stop four lanes of traffic, stood in the middle of the street, and sang into the bullhorn to the top of his voice. Everyone loved it. That was Dad. He always had fun and loved people. And they loved him.

When I would visit, he would pull me into the office to explain how his finances, insurances, and bills were organized and paid. I was not tuned in at first. After all, he was so healthy and mentally sharp, but he wanted me prepared just in case something happened to him. He had a "Cathy" inbox and discussed all the paperwork with me, then had me file it all away. I now understand that was his way of familiarizing me.

I finally realized he was serious, so I gave it priority when I visited. Each session I learned even more about him, his values and insights. I'm glad that I didn't waste those opportunities for a life lesson or sweet conversation. We chased a lot of rabbits sitting in that office. Later I was so glad that he pushed, and I learned, because neither of us ever dreamed that he would be struck with Huntington's disease.

Medicare's Not Free

My first introduction to Medicare insurance, health insurance supplements, and prescription costs began when he was sixty-five. He showed me his monthly premium books for each of them and explained that Medicare only paid about eighty percent of health costs, so he needed a supplement to pay the final twenty percent. There was no online bill-pay yet, so he wrote checks.

I was surprised that they had insurance premium payments each month and deductibles, but still had to pay for prescriptions out of pocket. Much later they received Medicare prescription insurance but still had a monthly premium and copays.

Like many young adults, I thought that Medicare was free healthcare. That's what they make you think, yes? Dad was still healthy and only went to the doctor for a yearly checkup. But for Mom it was priceless, and he emphasized the importance of their monthly health insurance payment. By the time he was seventy-two, I was listed on their accounts as an authorized point of contact.

In today's insurance market, Medicare is a tremendous value compared to hospital costs and individual insurance cost. But it's not free. Below is a quick overview, but I avoid details that would quickly be outdated. Refer to Medicare.gov for current information.

1. Medicare Part A (hospital costs) has no monthly premium but an annual deductible.
2. Part B (includes doctor visits) has a monthly premium, and an annual deductible.
3. Part C Advantage Plan has more affordable coverages but uses a designated network of hospitals and physicians.
4. Part D Prescription Insurance has monthly premiums, and some medications have a tiered copay.
5. Medicare supplement plans help pay for the 20 percent of costs not covered by Medicare. The supplement premium and coverages depend on the plan you choose.
6. Medicaid is a provision offered seniors and the disabled who cannot afford Medicare and have low income and savings. For eligibility information, see Medicare.gov.

Yes, Medicare and a supplement is much less than individual insurance and the healthcare is good, but it's not free. The costs and coverages change annually, so familiarize yourself with Medicare.gov.

In my forties, I had never thought about preparing for my parents' end-of-life years, much less my own. I don't even know what I assumed, but I'm glad that Dad insisted that I become familiar with their finances, and especially about the Medicare health insurance process. It made Clayton and me start organizing and planning early for our future health care.

The Transition

As Dad headed into confusion, he luckily became less interested. The office work was frustrating for him as his memory failed. He would occasionally ask how the money was doing, and I would say, "I do the bills online, just like you set them up."

"Oh, good."

If he asked about money I said, "You did a great job saving. You can live to a hundred." I always left extra cash in the account so I could show him.

He often wanted to go to the bank to get money, so we went inside to the teller for cash. The people at the bank thought he was so precious and loved it when he came. I helped him with his debit card, and he folded up the bills and put them in his wallet. I often wondered if going to the bank was habit or if he wanted to be sure there was money.

I could have gone through the ATM or given him cash or asked him why he needed money, but I wanted to give him respect or maybe just peace of mind.

Juggling Money

Whose money should be used? Are there savings, checking, annuities, retirement accounts, pensions, income from investments, or only social security? Which account should be used first? Living on a budget is a serious reality. It's a fixed income but with increasing health and living expenses. Should the children help pay for expenses so the parents' savings last longer? Or should a parent's bills be paid from their personal accounts first until depleted?

An elder law attorney in our state looked at my parents' accounts and expenses and developed a financial plan and budget. We were advised in our state to use all their savings first before contributing to their expenses.

We continued to use their bank account for the bills and their credit card for incidental expenses so the monthly statements could detail the income and expenditures. This accurate accounting was important for their taxes. When we were caring for our parents, though, there were always incidentals that we bought along with our daily purchases. That's just being a good daughter or son, and those costs were absorbed in our own cost of living. But when we kicked in significant funds, we kept a detailed record.

The early conversations and decisions helped me help them maintain their independence and quality of life. If your parents don't respond to the "help me help you" scenario, then you just let them keep control until… Sometimes there's nothing you can do. That's why early, early discussions are important to lay the groundwork.

Chapter 9

Home Care?

As a young man, Dad was always on the go. He was a great pastor, always the one in charge when he walked into a room. I could see his mind assessing. If a serving line was too long, he'd push around a few tables, add an extra line. When the church pews were getting full, he'd go to the podium and say, "SOS," which meant *slip over some*. If there was a person in need, they had his undivided attention. He spoke, people listened. People spoke, he cared.

At the church he pastored, there was a place for everyone. Young people, senior adults, special needs, children, married, single, wealthy, poor, hurting, broken, every background had a place and became family. Madeline and her husband were wealthy and every Sunday morning they ministered to special needs children so the parents could worship. Mr. J was poor, had no teeth, and wanted to be a greeter at the front door. No one stopped him. The church kids knew he had candy in his tattered coat pocket for them. This was not a typical church. It was lively and fun with dedicated people. Each Sunday lives were changed and families mended as people turned their hearts to God.

My mom, Lucille, was a bit quieter but still full of life. Everything centered on the Lord. Music was her niche, and on

Sunday, the organ was in full throttle as everyone poured in. She played the organ pedals with both feet, and sometimes the hymns took on the feel of a skating rink. The music lit up the sanctuary with a sense of anticipation. Voices were loud, handshakes exuberant, and singing lifted the roof. Those were great years and reflected the life they lived.

The Right Time for Home Care—When the Spouse is the Caregiver

In retirement, Dad's approach to Mom's care was much the same as his pastoring. He didn't call it in. He took full responsibility. Home was like a well-oiled machine. Organized and well planned. He cooked, cleaned, shopped, did laundry, the yard, planted flowers, paid bills. The pedal was down. When Mom was napping, he ran errands or tried to catch up on chores. Many Sundays, Mom was not well enough to go to church, but I knew Sunday was Dad's sweet spot and an opportunity to fellowship with friends. It was vital for his well-being.

When they moved to Jacksonville, we discussed hiring a caregiver for Sundays. It would be regularly scheduled so Dad could go early to the adult Bible study and then the church service. It worked wonderfully. The caregiver came from eight until one and assisted Mom with breakfast, dressing, and prepared lunch.

Eventually Dad couldn't leave Mom at all during the week. She was a fall risk and would randomly decide to cook or take a walk when he was gone. She locked herself out one day. Good thing it was Florida. So, we made the decision to add caregivers from nine until one Monday through Friday. Saturday was Cracker Barrel Day. But the hard truth was that there were still twenty hours left of caregiving each day.

Dad was still healthy and loved getting out, and I truly believe that this decision enhanced his quality of life for several more years. During those few hours, he drove to church, and there was always someone that wanted his attention. The pastor of the church and the staff pulled him in to the office for planning meetings or took him to lunch. It was just what he needed. On other days, he and his brother Bill ran errands and spent time together.

The Right Time for Home Care—When your Last Parent is Alone

Once a parent is living alone, their safety net is gone. I'm referring to someone that has eyes on them night and day. So now another family member should assume the role of contact. From this moment on, the decisions need to be a joint effort. The role of contact is the least invasive function as an adult child, but extremely essential. It's a safety mechanism and an assessment tool that the senior parent and adult child agree to. In a matter of hours, even a healthy senior can go from a fall or illness to critical condition if this step is neglected. So agree for them to have a call-in time morning and evening with family, or if they are active with just a reliable circle of friends.

My grandfather lived with us for a summer when I was a teenager. We had a rule that everyone must call in by ten p.m. if we were not going to be home. If I wanted my freedom, I knew to keep the deadline. My grandfather had to be reminded a few times, but the rule acted as a safety device for kids and adults coming and going. Remember the commercial, "It's ten o'clock. Do you know where your kids are?" For us it was Grandpa. Likewise, the morning/evening contact will provide everyone with peace of mind and the additional benefit of assessing any changes in behavior or personal needs.

So what triggers the home care? Both the physical and the mental capability will impact the timing and extent of home care. Some seniors don't know how or don't want to clean or cook. They may opt to have someone a few hours in the morning to make a meal, clean, or do laundry, especially if their spouse had fulfilled those duties previously. Other seniors are still driving and active enough to care for themselves, so the first step may be a weekly cleaning service. The important thing is that they are eating well, taking necessary medications, and have no mental confusion that would impact their safety.

A Life Alert pendant can be a pre-step before home care. In an emergency, the alert call center will have a list of nearby family or neighbors to contact first, or they will call 911 if necessary. Encourage your loved ones to press the pendant button for a practice call with the operator at least once a month so it will be a familiar, easy process if they need it.

The Finances—For Such a Time as This

When someone retires and the income flow comes to a halt, it's sobering. Social security is only a cushion, and Medicare with a supplement still has copays and premiums. So your livelihood becomes the lump-sum number on the statement in front of you. Divide that by the number of years ahead and you have your annual income. Best case scenario for my parents was comfortable, but the unknowns made Dad very insecure. He was a planner.

So asking him to spend money unnecessarily was a task. Starting home care one day a week put his toe in the water. He was free to let go for a few hours and breathe. He had no idea what a sense of relief it was. Before, when he left Mom alone, he was nervous and in a hurry to return. So one day a week was a gift.

Dad had savings, and even after retirement, he worked part-time for ten more years and saved much of it. We continued our conversations about the future. I asked him why he had saved money all those years. He said so he and Mom could have good care. For such a time as this.

Dad and Mom loved their home and church and living near his brothers. They had both grown up in North Florida, so they wanted to be there as long as they could manage. It was a good support system for the time and a great quality of life. Looking back, I can say that they stayed in their home to the very last possible day.

Agency or Friends?

Because Mom and Dad had a very supportive family and a very tight-knit church family, it could have been easy to find a person in the church to hire for their care. However, it was important to me, and you may feel the same, that things that happen at home, stay at home. Their privacy and dignity needed to be preserved so they could enjoy their family and church family.

The second reason to keep a separation was the professional rapport that should be established. Even though you can develop a loving relationship with caregivers, you may not feel as free to change caregivers or have crucial conversations if they are friends and family. It could get touchy.

I also discovered that the benefit for using an agency is the vetting, training, and insurance provided. An agency also has backup caregivers if your caregiver is ill or takes a vacation. I called a local Visiting Angels franchise, and the owner came, met my parents, and discussed exactly what was needed. Mom needed a shower and dressing each morning and the room straightened up. Twice a week the laundry would need to be done and the sheets on the bed changed weekly. The caregiver would also need to cook their main meal at lunch. Because the agency was a franchise, the owner took personal interest in every client. It took a few tries before we found the exact person, and I didn't hesitate to change caregivers.

The caregivers had to administer medications, so a single-day pillbox was placed out each morning. She was also allowed to give Tylenol. All the other medications were locked up and out of sight.

The Right Caregiver for Mom

Mom was becoming very childlike and was occasionally agitated. Sharon walked into our lives at just the right moment. She was a sweet, caring woman that knew exactly how to handle my mother. She would baby her and talk sweetly to her and could get Mom to do anything. Whew, what a gift. My mother was at great peace when Sharon walked in, and so we let her take over.

Crucial Conversation with a Caregiver

Sharon came in one day crying. Her husband had left her, and she was a mess. My parents are naturally compassionate and let her talk and talk, then prayed with her. The next few weeks, Sharon was sullen, moody, and teary. It was bringing the whole family down every day.

I came down for a week and experienced a few days with her. Knowing that this could not continue but wanting to be compassionate, I told her that I was sorry for what she was going through. I explained that our family was at a critical time in our lives, and it took all we could do to keep our heads above water. I needed her to place all her burdens at the front door, walk in with joy, and lift the spirits of our household every day. It would also do her good to lay her sorrow aside for four hours and lift her own spirits. She said she would try.

The next morning, a smiling lady bounced in the front door and turned on the joy. It changed all of us. At the end of that day, she hugged me and said it had improved her whole outlook on life and helped her children at home. I could have just let her go, but I wanted to give her a chance to turn it around for her sake and ours.

I believe that God brought her into our lives at a critical time, and God also used us to help her. Sharon was with us for three years until my parents moved to live with us in Pennsylvania. Four years later, she appeared at my mom's funeral in Jacksonville. We had a tearful hug, and words weren't necessary.

The Right Caregiver for Dad

My parents lived with us for several years in Pennsylvania before my mom went to heaven. Then there was one. It was only Dad to care for. He was getting more unsteady but did well with showering, shaving, and dressing himself. I took him out with me each day, but he tired easily. Clayton and I talked about finding a caregiver for three days a week. We also needed time to go see our children and grandchildren occasionally, so we wanted to establish a relationship with a caregiver.

A colleague of Clayton's had just lost his wife to Alzheimer's and told us about his wonderful caregiver that had been with them for five years. We contacted her and were thrilled at the interview. Paola was a senior citizen, intelligent, kind, and articulate. Really a godsend to us. She came from ten until three, three days a week, and would keep his clothes cleaned and pressed, his room straightened, and lunch made. It evolved into a sweet relationship for Dad and a great support and friend for me.

One day, I came home about two o'clock and they were still sitting at the lunch table talking up a storm. Paola jumped up and apologized for not having the laundry done and the kitchen cleaned from lunch. I told her that the most important task for her was to spend time with Dad. The other things were incidental to the time talking and sharing. So they did. She was masterful about asking the right questions, and he spent hours each day telling her the story of his life and about his family growing up. Many days while she pressed his shirts, they watched the Gaither videos that Dad had accumulated, or they would sit at the computer, and she would help him read and respond to his many Facebook friends. He had more than I did.

Paola was a dear friend to me. One day I slipped out of the

house without saying goodbye to my dad, and she had a discussion with me about it. She looked out for him and taught me good lessons along the way. Paola had left her career years earlier to care for her own parents until they died, then she decided to stay in home care. We shared a lot about life for those few years. She was just the dignified, caring, soft-spoken person that we all needed. Isn't God good?

Chapter 10

Manage the Meds

Make it easy on yourself

At the age of ninety-one, my father had been on Prilosec (omeprazole) for over fifteen years. When he missed a day or two of taking it, he would experience burning reflux. It was a simple over-the-counter medication, and I had not given it much thought until the doctor mentioned that he should probably change it. Dad was ninety-one. Why? He felt great. The medicine did its job, and he was miserable when he missed a dose.

The doctor told me that Prilosec should only be taken for fourteen days. What? It had been over fifteen years. Maxwell Smart would snap his fingers and say, "Missed it by *that* much." Dad was ninety-one, and we're going to change that medication now? A medication that he had taken since he was seventy-five and was miserable without. I didn't even know what to say. I didn't know which was worse, not catching it for fifteen whole years, or wanting to take it away at age ninety-one.

There are so many issues in that story I don't know where to begin. How many doctors, pharmacists, and PAs saw it listed for years? The truth is, I didn't even look at the information pamphlet either. So at that point, I chose for him to stay on the medication.

I just want to add that if Dad had been on that medication less than a year, or if he had a long life ahead of him, or if he was having side effects from it, I would have made the adjustment. But I chose quality of life. Comfort.

So, it's important to have your doctor look at all the medications every time. Some of the meds will be from other doctors, but still look at and discuss each one. Determine if there are two for the same thing, and one could be eliminated. Maybe there is a new medication that combines them both. Maybe there is a new treatment with fewer long-term side effects. You want each doctor to know and analyze all the medications with you. By doing this process, you will learn from the doctors, and often they learn from your observations.

Knowing the Medications

Develop a common sense approach with only a few facts from the drug information sheet or online (i.e., webmd.com). They both provide this information in seconds. I also realize that the information here is basic and may be a refresher.

1. Name of Medication: There are often two names for the same medication, a brand name and generic name. The generic, less expensive medication is available after the original brand name has been on the market long enough to recoup its research and development costs. The price difference can be enormous.
2. Conditions Treated by the Medication: Example: Lowers blood pressure, treats infections, relieves a cough, etc. Or a secondary use: Can prevent migraines.
3. Side Effects of Medication: Reading about the most common side effects such as nausea, drowsiness, and headache can make you aware of a possible reaction.

4. Strength and Daily Dose of the Medication: Know the dose. Most medications are capsules or tablets measured in milligrams (Mg) or micrograms (Mcg).
5. How Long and When to Take the Medications: Ask the doctor or pharmacist if any of the medications interact and need to be taken separately. Note that if a medication causes drowsiness, ask if you can take it at night, or if you have trouble sleeping, change a medication to the morning. Vitamins can also keep you awake or make you relax.
6. Food and Water: Some medications recommended to take with a meal or on an empty stomach (usually morning). But before you assume a medication doesn't work or causes a side effect, just add water. Drink a full glass of water to dissolve the pill completely and enhance its effectiveness.
7. Questions to ask when adding new medication to your routine:

- Can you start only one new medication at a time? If you start two new medications and have a reaction, you won't know which one caused the side effect, whether it be rash, drowsiness, nausea, stomach upset, headache, or difficulty breathing.
- Can you start the new medication at a half dose, and if there are no negative reactions, then increase it to full dose?
- When should the medication start working? After you are on a full dose, sometimes it takes weeks for it to get into your system. So watch for benefits or side effects to become more apparent as time passes.

Are you getting the common sense? The doctor will give you feedback about easing into the medication or a good reason to

take it immediately. It is a good learning opportunity either way. Remember, you go home and put this into your body.
 You live with this.

Less Is More

Doctors genuinely want to make you well. You made an appointment with the expectation of finding a remedy. The doctor feels that expectation. You tell them your symptoms, or they get test results, and because they have studied medicine, they use what they know to address your needs. So medications continue to be added each time you have an additional health symptom. As we know, sometimes you feel the side effects from a medication, then another medication is added to combat that side effect, and it goes on and on.

 Another contributor is having more than one doctor, and most of us do. Each one prescribes medications, and we end up with pills that may overlap or have interactions. The result is being overmedicated.

Health List—Don't Leave Home without It

The absolute most valuable tool is the health list. It is information at my fingertips that is easy to maintain, including everything needed at a doctor's office, hospital visit, or 911 emergency such as personal information, medical history, medications, and physicians. I kept a hard copy by the door and a digital one on my phone. The physician's response was, "Wow, this is great. I wish everyone would do this." Once the data is on a computer, it's easy to update from anywhere.

Walk with Me

Health List
Updated: January 2022
LINDA ANN ALEXANDER
DOB: July 10, 1944

Emergency Contact:
Your Name:
Your Address:
Your Cell Number:

MEDICATIONS AND SUPPLEMENTS

Glipizide	Diabetes	250 mg	2x (breakfast and supper)	Pink/oblong 93
Omeprazole	Acid reflux	20 mg	1x (before breakfast)	Red/oblong 20
Armour Thyroid	Low thyroid	60 mg	1x (before breakfast)	Beige/round A
Gabepentin	Nerve pain	100 mg	3x (breakfast, lunch, bed)	Yellow cap
Vitamin D3	Low D3	5000 IU	1x (bed)	Soft gel

ALLERGIES: Sulfa drugs—cause rash. Codine—causes nausea, vomiting

HEALTH CONDITIONS: Diabetes, peripheral neuropathy

SURGERIES: Gall bladder, 2001; Knee replacement, 2009

PHYSICIANS

Primary care: Doctor's name and phone number
OBGYN: Doctor's name and phone number
Endocrinologist: Doctor's name and phone number

PHARMACIES

MedicareRX: Phone number
CVS Pharmacy: Phone number

Health List

The health list is basic information, and at first, was created for the caregivers. If they had an emergency, all the information would be on one page. Then I realized it was helpful for organizing and ordering the medications, because some days I'd look at a pill and couldn't remember what it was for.

Every time you update the health list, change the current date in the heading. More important, save the previous lists for a paper trail of physicians and medications. You'll refer to it often for the date a med was taken, the dosage, or if it was ever prescribed, etc.

Take a paper copy of the health list to doctor's appointments and review each medication. It makes the doctor sit beside you and talk. Some medications are meant to treat a short-term problem, but the pharmacy puts them on autofill. The doctor will catch mistakes if you are looking together, but the greatest benefit is that it promotes discussion. The health list has more than just medicine. It has everything. As the years progress, you will rely on it more.

Prescription ordering has come a long way. Now the physician calls them in, and most pharmacies will text you when the prescription is ready. Then the pharmacy will automatically refill it each month.

Even easier, MedicareRx prescriptions will mail three months of basic medications right to your door. The mail order prescriptions are much cheaper, and some basic ones are free. When you set up your parents' online profile, the prescriptions are all listed. Just a click on a box, and they will be at your door in a few days. The online service will also contact your physician when a new refill prescription is needed.

Be sure to call and ask the MedicareRx representative how to become listed on the account as a designated/approved contact to order on their behalf. If you have any question about how to set it up or order, you can call the 800 number. Amazingly enough, they always answer quickly and can pull up the account and walk you through the process. They can tell you how much a medication costs, when it can be reordered, and can connect you with a pharmacist if you have a medication question.

I ordered my parents' medications from my house every month for a year, then when the medication arrived, Dad verified the order with me. Just a safety hint: We made sure that all medication bottles were kept out of sight. A trusted caregiver would know where they were, but people coming in and out of the house could not see any pill bottles.

Home Medication Organization

When I first noticed the problem, there were two prescription bottles for Dad and five for Mom sitting on the kitchen counter. Some had to be taken three times a day, others just at night, others at noon and bedtime. At meals, Dad would open each bottle and put pills by their plate. A good process for then.

Later, on one of my visits, I noticed Mom fiddling with the medication bottles at random times during the day. That's when it got touchy. "Hey Mom, whatcha' doin'?"

The reply was, "I'm not feeling very good, so I'm taking a pill."

Now it got touchier. "I'm sorry you feel bad. Can I help?"

Too late. Down the hatch, and it was gone. Scared me. I admit that I wanted to grab her and make her spit it out or cough it up. But I figured it wasn't the first time, and she had apparently lived.

The problem was that I'd never had to tattle on my mom before. New territory. I had to have a critical conversation and help Dad not to overreact like I wanted to. I was sitting close to him in the office and blocking him in until I got finished, and we came up with a plan. It scared him.

Things were changing, and it was a whole new ball game.

Long story short, Dad quickly learned that we had to be precise with the medications. We looked online and purchased seven-day pill boxes, Sunday through Saturday. Each day had a section for morning, noon, evening, and bedtime pills. Dad started putting the pills for the week in the pill boxes and placing all the other medications in a duffle bag in the top of the closet.

Yes, there was a tug of war between them for a while. You see, Mom had taken medication her whole life, and she didn't understand why it had to change. There was no reasoning with her. My dear mom was becoming childlike. You'll laugh at all the crazy things we did to appease her, like putting children's vitamins in her pill bottle so she could have some control. Mom was so sweet, and it was important not to hurt her feelings.

Finally I had to figure out how to end the daily struggle for my dad. Eventually I purchased a small combination safe to put on a kitchen shelf inside the cupboard. It held a one-week pill box and Dad's two prescriptions bottles. We spent a week talking out loud with Mom about the dangers of a stranger getting into the medications. We talked about all the ways we could lock them up. She was part of the conversations and agreed that we should keep the medications safely out of sight.

When I brought in the small safe and put it in the cupboard, she helped locate the perfect spot and was part of the process. Whew. It seemed to work. It made sense to her. We were always thinking how to balance safety, dignity, happiness, and quality of life. Yes, she asked for the combination, and I told her. She didn't remember it, and never asked again. That was it.

As both of my parents' health declined, I ordered the medication online or by phone from my home. Every three months, Medicare Rx would deliver to their front door. When I visited, I would fill four to eight weeks' worth of pill boxes. It had become too tedious for my dad as his mind was beginning to decline.

To be honest, I had to concentrate also. The health list with the medications was my guide, and I updated it as needed.

Sometimes all I had to do was change the date at the top and adjust the medications on the health list. But the cool thing was that in only an hour, all the medications were in pill boxes and the health list was updated. It was done.

If your parents live alone, there are pill timers to remind them when to take their medications. There are also pharmacies that will pre-package the pills for morning, noon, and night in separate packets. You will become creative in your approach to medication ordering and organization. Just make it easy on yourself. There must be an app for that.

Just to recap, the pill boxes are a lifesaver. In an hour, several months' supply of medications can be organized. Otherwise, it is daily opening and closing and putting away bottles, looking at the doses and times to make sure it is right. It cuts down the chances of error and increases the ease of taking the medications consistently. If you can't remember if you took a dose, it's clear because the pills are still in the pill box. It can slip into a purse or pocket for a day out or for a meal out. You can make up an extra day to keep in the car. You can grab a week's worth if there is an emergency.

Chapter 11

The Mind Is an Interesting Thing

Their mind still loves, fears, longs for their spouse, and has glimpses of their past

A song by Casting Crowns tells about relationships fading, but I always think of memory loss when I hear it. It's also a slow fade, a relationship crumbling away. Our parents developed various degrees of confusion, childishness, agitation, personality change, or memory decline. What was unexpected? The personal toll on us.

The Mind Is a Personal Battle

It's hard to watch, different from physical decline. Even though you know where it's heading, you can't predict exactly how or when. Adjusting to that next level of incapability is personal. It's emotional. Thankfully, the person with memory loss doesn't always feel the loss, but you do. Life changes progressively—who they are now, who you are together. It's a slow fade. Relationship crumbles into a new temporary.

Growing up, when I would face a task, Mom would say, "Roll up your sleeves, put your hair behind your ears, pick 'em up, put 'em down!" Usually, I was standing over a sink of dishes. Her voice stayed in my head. "Be strong and get to work."

My emotions would swing from despair to laughing my head off. Humor was a respite from frustration. I didn't want to look back with regrets, wishing I hadn't yelled, hurt their feelings, or developed resentments. So the strange and funny episodes were embraced.

Discovering the strength of scripture, the melodies of worship, and the calm of prayer put life into perspective, to get the most out of today. This time is not something to just get through. I challenge you to live it, sleeves rolled up, hair behind your ears.

The Mind Is a Task Changer

Did you know that mental deterioration changes daily living? Every run-of-the-mill activity evolves into a new set of decisions, adjusting the when and how of everything. How they buy groceries, cook, open the mail, order and take medications, need care, attend doctors' appointments, plan holidays, answer phone calls, communicate and reason, clean house, shop, handle finances, drive, shower and dress, and last but not least, safety.

The Mind Can Be Frustrating

The mind has a mind of its own. In every fading mind, dreams are still dreamed, stories are still told, imaginations create fantasies, and scrambled facts go unnoticed. Minds remain active.

It's normal to become frustrated, but correcting mistaken facts, dates, or people only produces worry. In fact, joining them in the tales of their imagination creates opportunities to connect. Comfort instead of correct, divert with a delicious sweet, a change of subject, or a stroll outside, to soothe a troubled mind.

Dad still knew he was a pastor. He wasn't sure where he was, but his mind still felt the pressure of preparing a sermon or visiting the sick. One day he was worried about preaching on Sunday, so I told him, "Pastor Burkholder got the word that you needed him. Do you want him to preach from now on?" Dad was so relieved, "Oh, yes. Would he?" Another time he asked me if the missionaries were all right. So I recalled some of the names, and we talked about them. His mind was his memories, his memories were ministry, his ministry was his heart. It was his happy place. God did that.

The Mind Changes Personality

Remember, it's not them. You'll need to say this to yourself. This personality is not your parent. They look like your parent, but you can't reason with them, or they may be agitated or childish. It's not them.

I observed a wife in memory care accidently use the name of her first husband. Her present husband was hurt and furious, but she didn't understand what she said. It was him she was calling. It was him that she reached for. He couldn't ignore it, chuckle about it, or love her through it. "She wants you," I wanted to tell him.

The Mind Is a Funny Thing

I was on "Jack watch" at his and Lola's condo. His dementia made him often confused. Lola was having surgery, so Brian and Clayton were at the hospital. Remember, Jack was in a wheelchair, only one leg. Understandably, he was antsy, agitated, and wanted to go to the hospital. I diverted his attention all morning, but he was smoking mad and caught me with a right punch that landed. He wheeled himself outside for some fresh air.

A few minutes later, I heard the neighbors calling for me to come quickly. I grabbed my purse and bolted into the parking lot. I stepped outside just as Jack parked his wheelchair, hopped beside the car, and sat in the driver's seat. He had the keys to the car. Calmly, I opened the driver's door. "Hey Pop, want me to drive?"

"Why, sure girlie!"

Whew, that could have gone several ways. Jack got out of the car with a hop, hop, hop, around to the passenger side as I loaded the wheelchair in the trunk. I waved a thank you to the congregated neighbors.

That's my funny Jack story, and I chuckle at the scene now, even though it wasn't quite as amusing then. I let his sons wrestle with him the rest of the day at the hospital. So to sum it up, I was punched by an old man in a wheelchair, got outsmarted, and entertained the neighborhood, all in one morning.

The Mind-Altering Elements

Some behaviors are not just old age but caused by physical trauma, medication, infection, or surroundings. So look for a root cause if the mental change or confusion is sudden.

Lola was mentally sharp into her late eighties. Her physical frailties required a nursing home her last two years. One morning when I popped in for a visit, Lola was alert and sitting tall on the edge of the bed, which was unusual. She motioned me to come in quickly. "Hurry, I'm glad you came early. Something's afoot!" She had this strange look in her eyes. "Those girls out there are up to no good and need to be reported."

Normally I would take her seriously, but everything about her was off. I had to appease her. "Okay, I'll go out, look around, and check things out. You rest, and I'll be right back."

I went to the nurses' station and asked them to check her out. They discovered a fever from a UTI. It made her talk out of her head, which is common with urinary tract infections in seniors. The caregivers were so used to aging patients being off, they didn't compare it with her normal state.

Lola was taken to the emergency room for IV antibiotics and

admitted to the hospital. With a few hours of IV fluids, she was back to herself and didn't even remember me coming to her room. Since then, I've added *something's afoot* to my vocabulary. It comes in handy.

The Mind Is Childlike

My mom, Lucille, was thoughtful and quiet. Dad was upbeat and always busy. But the last few years, they switched personalities as their minds changed. Mom wanted activities, and Dad sat still and quiet.

My role also altered. I became the parent, first with Mom as she became childlike and her ability to reason decreased. Every task, activity, in fact every word, had to be well thought out, often on the fly.

The mysterious thing was that her long-term memory was sharp. In fact, one day we were talking about getting new glasses. She said, "We ought to call Dr. Gwaltney where you got your first contacts." What? I was sixteen. I could never have recalled his name. The mind is an interesting thing.

Mom, however, wasn't capable of the easiest puzzle. She didn't get the concept of corner pieces or flat edged pieces or matching colors. It just wouldn't compute, yet she could fill in the gaps to a story from forty years ago.

Then there was sundown syndrome. It barged its way into our afternoons with discontentment, sadness, or agitation. I learned quickly that in late afternoon, she became disoriented. I tried everything. About four o'clock, I'd turn on all the lights in the house, put on happy music, and get mom occupied with some activity to divert attention away from whatever was bothering her.

Years later when my dad was in memory care, I noticed it happened like clockwork to the residents. Near sundown, the patients walking the halls or sitting in the activity room would be uncooperative or despondent. One person would start crying or arguing and others would join in. It was uncanny.

The Mind Knows

Through it all, there are innate qualities in people that still remain at the core. Lucille grew up as a PK (preacher's kid) and had scripture read to her every day. Her heart was permeated by her faith. When I was a child, I saw her sitting with her Bible and reading. Living with me, she had her little nest of things beside her recliner—coffee cup, Bible, glasses, note pad, and pen. She scribbled prayers, made plans, and wrote ideas that made sense only to her. Her heart and mind knew God during those precious moments, and it was just as real at eighty-six.

The Mind Deteriorates

We both knew how this would go, the Huntington's disease and Dad's mind deteriorating. We had seen it firsthand with my grandma, the mental and physical decline. The difference was that Dad was late seventies at onset and Grandma was the usual forty. The initial sorrow had passed for Dad, and his awareness of his decline lessened. I was glad for that. He didn't fret about it and remained involved in life.

But there was a natural progression to the decline. I discovered that new undertakings were not possible, but the daily, repetitive tasks remained. For example, he didn't know what to do with new pieces of mail, but he loved sitting for hours in his office reading Facebook. He made oatmeal and toast for breakfast every morning a long time after other abilities had ceased. He bathed, shaved, and dressed independently until his fall at eighty-nine.

During his last five years, he quit watching television or movies because he couldn't follow the story line. He looked at the newspaper but wasn't reading it. Later I realized that his mind looped about every five minutes, erasing his short-term memory. I know this because he fell and a few minutes later he didn't remember. He was in a state of confusion, and there were times he would mention that his mind wasn't right. I am glad I realized what it was because it helped me understand and comfort him.

What was shocking to me was that everything changed the day he fell and broke his hip. He was eighty-nine. He woke up from surgery disoriented, and his mind was never clear again. Up to that day, he loved to reminisce about childhood and join in conversations. But after that, he was incapable of a conversation, just simple thoughts. I realized one day that he couldn't recognize words or write his name. Those milestones marked the path for me. For the next two years, he talked less and less, but we communicated. Words weren't necessary.

The Mind Gives Gifts

Dad had not spoken much in his last weeks. I pulled a chair near his recliner to sit closer. He took a deep breath and said, "We've had a great life, haven't we?"

Shocked, I answered, "We sure did, Dad. You gave me the best life. You were a great father."

"I was?"

"Oh yes, and I love you so much."

"I love you too," and he patted my hand. That was it. I mean, that was the last talk from him to me, from me to him.

I called Clayton and said, "I got a real gift today."

Dad remembered my name right to the end. When he spotted me coming into memory care each day, his face would light up, he would clap his hands together and say, "There's Cathy!" Then he would introduce me to the caregivers, almost every day. "This is my daughter!"

Don't miss the gifts. Even when your loved one's mind has faded far away, there are brief moments of awakenings. It may be a penetrating look, a meaningful word, or an intentional touch that will connect your hearts. They are cherished moments you keep.

Their mind still loves, fears, longs for their spouse, and has glimpses of their past. And they know that your face, familiar or forgotten, belongs to them.

Chapter 12

You're Not Superman
Caring's toll

I pulled away, Dad standing outside Mom's rehab. It had been a three-week visit in Jacksonville. A severe fall, surgery, and two more weeks of rehab ahead. I felt like a heel leaving Dad exhausted to carry on alone, but I needed to drive to Palm Beach to see family.

The next morning my son, Ryan, asked if I could watch my four-year-old granddaughter for the day, and I felt it would be a good break for me. When I picked her up, she asked to go see Grandma Lola. I used my key to open Lola's door and called for her. There was a faint cry, and I rushed into her bedroom. Lola had been ill all night and had fallen on the floor. Her Life Alert necklace was around her neck, unused. I immediately called 911, and within an hour I was standing by her bed in the ER, still toting my granddaughter on my hip.

The day was long and exhausting by the time Lola was admitted and moved upstairs. When my daughter, Celeste, came in, she immediately thought I was having a stroke because the right side of my face and mouth was drooping severely. Brian arrived to stay with Lola, and Ryan came to get my granddaughter.

I felt fine but went downstairs to the ER. No stroke or heart problem. It was diagnosed as Bell's Palsy. They asked me if I had been under any stress lately. I laughed.

To be truthful, I didn't feel stressed, just torn about leaving my dad, but I wouldn't have called it stress. So what was it? It was trying to be everywhere at once. Yes, it was stress.

Bell's Palsy? I looked bizarre. All the women will understand. Don't mess with my face. I was sent to a specialist and put on a strong concoction of prednisone and anti-inflammatories. It took four weeks until my eye, cheek, and lip were not drooping. I learned that it could come back, so every time I feel a twinge in my face, I jump into deep-slow breathing, which stresses me out.

There is a funny part to this. About the third day, I saw a doctor friend of ours with a dry sense of humor. I thought he would be sympathetic and give me some medical advice or hope. He said, "Don't worry. No one will notice. Halloween is this week."

Finding the Balance

Years later, when Mom and Dad lived with us, Clayton would say, "You can't make them happy every waking hour." He was right. No one is happy every waking hour. Happiness wasn't my job; love and good care was. As circumstances changed with the parents' care, I learned to settle in and take time to renew. Get someone to share the care.

Taking care of you is not selfish, especially when you're so vital to the health and well-being of your loved one. I needed care physically, mentally, emotionally, and spiritually.

So, I had to make decisions to do one or two things each day for my own health. The Bell's Palsy was a warning. Here's how I started.

A Sense of Well-being

Physically, I'm not superman, but I've always been healthy. However, I realized that physical activity improved my mental and emotional well-being. Did I say workout or exercise? No, just moving, changing my surroundings, and getting my heart pumping. Now if you love the gym or your treadmill, even better. But I wanted to actually enjoy it, so I either took a long walk or went to the mall. Don't laugh; I walked rather briskly between the shops and took the stairs up to the next level.

Think about what you enjoy. Walking, gardening, dancing, taking a drive, hiking, going to the driving range, biking, or even rocking on the porch. It doesn't have to be hours, just twenty minutes in different surroundings. I did realize, however, that it required intentional scheduling because I obviously didn't know I was stressed until too late.

Mentally, I was a bit paranoid, especially watching my parents' mental decline and knowing that I could be a candidate for Huntington's disease. So, I signed into our bank account quite often just to check that I remembered the ridiculously long username and password. But seriously, my mind was in care mode all the time, and I needed mental distraction and stimulation.

My daughter tricked me into joining the online game, Words with Friends. It was addictive, and I had games going with Celeste and an odd array of friends. I also made time for a soft chair and my book, or a mystery movie. What things do you enjoy that takes your total concentration? Add that in.

Emotionally, I was changing. Remember the girl who seldom shed a tear? Well, this road made me emotional. Yes, Clayton was still the tenderhearted weeper in the family, but my eyes teared easier now. We found that maintaining our normal routine with date night and activities with friends was more difficult, but it was key to our emotional health.

One of our most difficult decisions was to have our normal vacation each year and to visit our children regularly. Some of the times were shorter, but our relationships were vital to our well-being. We had family or caregivers stay with our parents when we left town and backups to our backups just in case. Time away was priceless for me, and I came back stronger.

It's about an emotional tank. When we see a wife struggling, we say, "The marbles are out of her jar; her emotional jar is empty." Because when someone loves us or cares for us, it puts marbles in our jar. In a love relationship, we do it for each other every day. Marbles go in each other's jar with a hug, love note, or time together until it fills up.

Marbles go out of the jar with loneliness, verbal abuse, or indifference. Slowly over time, the filled jar gets empty and hits a marriage crisis. Believe me, I kept a handful of marbles for Clayton during this time because my focus was divided. When we got short with each other, we planned time away to reconnect. We learned valuable lessons during this time that made our marriage stronger.

After the Bell's Palsy, I also had to gauge my emotional health in a different way. I took a day each week to get a monthly massage or spend time with friends with no talk of caregiving. Just eat my favorite comfort food, laugh, and talk about them and everything else. I had neglected friends but didn't realize it and paid a price.

Spiritual health is more than church on Sunday. Yes, it's the foundation, but I found healing for my soul in a quiet time or a devotion. A thirty-minute video Bible study from my church became my spiritual nourishment (cc-chestersprings.com). The pastor sits on a stool, opens his Bible, prays, and I take a deep breath and let the prayer wash over me. With my Bible and pen in hand, I take a dive into the Word. I've been going to church all my life, but these verse-by-verse studies added a new dimension to my walk with God and again made me stronger.

Sustaining the balance of physical, mental, emotional, and spiritual well-being is the calm but intentional approach I need. It feeds the body, soul, and spirit.

Chapter 13

Developing Partnerships
Doctors, specialists, nurses

My dermatologist is excellent. No personality, but a perfectionist. I want a perfectionist in a dermatologist. The only smile I ever got out of him was when I apologized for not ironing my birthday suit. I got chuckles from the assistant, but only the corner of his mouth turned up. My friend had cancer on his ear and a chunk had to be cut out. This dermatologist spent hours getting his ear to look perfect, and it does. So I will take his perfection over the lack of personality any time.

Anyway, I called one day because a spot turned up on my forehead and got an appointment with the PA. She was great. Took it off in a sliver and no pain whatsoever. She had a great personality, and we talked the entire time. I've developed a relationship with the PA. Now I call for her when I need something zapped or quickly removed, but I see him for checkups—minus the jokes.

Physician's Contract with Society

In the Philadelphia airport is an area of rocking chairs near the food court. It's a perfect place to sit and observe passengers and crews. Of course, the pilots are most interesting. They have a certain swagger as they walk, decked out in their uniforms. After all, they have the lives of hundreds of people in their hands every day, and that's why they walk with confidence. It's quite impressive and oddly enough, I trust these strangers with my life.

We often attribute the confidence of our physicians with having a similar swagger or God complex. They, too, impact life and death. Actually, there used to be an unspoken contract between society and our physicians. If they go to medical school for years, graduate in the top of their class, emerge under a great burden of debt, complete a grinding residency, commit to on-call for life, then they will receive a lucrative salary, get the best tables at restaurants, and be highly respected by society. Sadly, those days of high esteem and lucrative salaries have passed.

Now the physicians' costs have skyrocketed, and their reimbursements have declined. Their personal debt and their liability insurances are crippling. They see so many patients every hour that both are shortchanged. They wear their white coats and are truly dedicated to healing. Yet movie stars, athletes, and musicians make millions to entertain, while physicians make far less to heal and save lives.

So how do you merge your need for good care and the physician's pressure to maintain their practice? You need a doctor, RN, or PA that will engage. You need to develop a real relationship with someone in that office.

When my parents lived in Jacksonville, I lived in Palm Beach. I was with them for many of their appointments in Jacksonville. I met Rita, the RN for their primary care physician. She knew that I closely looked after them. If I called the office, she would always return my call, sometime that day. Eventually Rita would call me whenever they came in for an appointment on their own, and she also called me when she got their blood work or test results back. We became real friends through it all. I made a point to brag about her to the doctor and send her thank you notes.

The HIPAA laws prevent anyone having access to your parents' medical information. Having a medical power of attorney is vital as your parents age. Otherwise, they require verbal permission each time you speak to their health professionals. Dad gave permission over the phone to list me as an authorized contact. Chapter 21 discusses important documents and preparations for transitioning responsibility.

Trust but Verify—It's Your Life

Should you trust your doctor? Yes, you should. At least as much, perhaps a lot more, than the pilot of your plane. You also have a personal responsibility to verify by asking questions and managing your own health. You already manage your housing, food, exercise, clothing, family, education, entertainment, finances, relationships, and faith. What if you didn't pay attention to your family, forgot to pay your bills, wore your sweats every day, or didn't bother to get an education? Your life would be in crisis. When you stop and think about it, your health is the important function that allows you to do all those activities.

If you blindly walk into the doctor's office, listen without understanding, ingest whatever medication is prescribed, you chance an outcome of uncertainty. Or even worse, if you avoid wellness checks, ignore troubling symptoms, and hope for the best, you will experience a mess. That's not a medical or technical term, but it best describes the results.

There are over three hundred million people in the United States, and not one of us is the same. We are unique in everything from our DNA to our personalities to our emotions. So we are fortunate that physicians have norms and best practices that can quickly diagnose, recommend treatment, and deliver care. That means the majority of the population will respond well and recover because of the years of research, development, and practice of the most common illnesses. Healthcare treats the masses, so statistically we can get the best result. You see where I am going with this?

However, first we are required to provide accurate information, and second, we learn to observe. Just like everything else in life, we are responsible to manage the basics of our health.

The Right Fit–Primary Care, Specialist, Physician's Assistant, Nurse

Describe the perfect doctor. Happy personality, caring bedside manner, produces quality outcomes, experienced, with plenty of time. I could add mind reader. These are all the characteristics you look for in your doctor. We expect them to be an Avenger hero with the personality of Mother Teresa. How do we find a physician that is the right fit for us and our loved ones? I finally found a good combination for each, and each one is vital to the whole picture.

Let's picture walking into a modern New York musical theater. You locate a soft chair and push down the padded seat. You settle in and notice the people dressed in black, carrying a variety of instruments, filing onto the stage and forming an orchestra.

Dissonant sounds begin with ascending scales, a series of staccato tones, and loud deep blasts from horns. It's an inharmonious moment. You're wondering, *How could this be?* You know that these professionals have spent money on their beloved instruments, years of tedious practice to perform tonight. Then a first chair musician or pianist stands and plays a single note. This musician, with an imperceptible hand motion, unifies the dissonant sounds to one tone.

As the conductor appears onstage, the crowd applauds. He knows the body of music, and though he is not proficient in each instrument, he knows the mechanics of each one. Most important, he knows how the body of work is to sound and the individual part each musician plays. He sees the whole and the parts.

Like a conductor, your primary care physician knows the whole body and should take the lead in your health. Your primary physician will use instruments such as blood work, health history, symptoms, and medications to keep your body in tune. But if there are occasions that a condition or age requires a screening, your primary doctor has a complete orchestra of specialists that focuses on one area all day, every day.

But even the world-renowned health systems don't always manage well. It's assumed that everyone is working together. Not necessarily true. Yes, it's great to have numerous specialists in one place, but there must be one physician with all the results on one page. Without it, each specialist prescribes a medication or treatment, and patients become over-medicated and over-doctored.

Primary Care Physician—Come Prepared

How do you find your conductor? Usually, it will be your primary care doctor unless you have a chronic condition and see your specialist the most. Your conductor does need to be someone that sees you and remembers you and knows your story. A primary doctor taking the lead is the one point of contact, the conductor.

Quite often the physician takes the lead during the appointment, so being prepared with notes about what you need is crucial. Otherwise, you are answering the doctor's questions, getting examined, prescribed medications, and you leave without telling them health or medication problems. Many older adults can't answer the doctor's questions and when they return home don't remember what the doctor said or why they have new medications. So come prepared or have an advocate who will remember the questions and answers.

1. Be the main doctor: Tell your primary care doctor that you want them to be your conductor. When you have an illness, you would rather have your primary doctor treat you whenever possible. It eliminates redundant doctors' appointments and makes life easier.
2. Prepare notes: Bring the health list and questions about medications, symptoms, or reasons why you're there. Is each medication still necessary? Less is more.
3. Have an advocate: If you, a spouse, or your parent is sick, make sure someone accompanies them that can remember and can communicate with the doctor. Occasionally, I have even been on speaker phone when my parents had their appointment. Permission for me to receive health information and speak on their behalf is on file. That's the beauty of a good physician partnership.

Physician's Assistants and Nurses—MVPs

Physician's assistants have turned out to be my go-to person, my MVPs. The PA of the primary care physician could become your conductor. They are qualified to do many of the physician's tasks, and I have found that a physician's assistant enjoys the patient contact and engages easier. If you call the office and ask for the physician's assistant, generally they will return your call or see you in the office or at least talk to the doctor and take care of you.

Clayton's mom, Lola, was in a nursing home her last year. Penny was the physician's assistant from Dr. J's office and was our conductor. Dr. J had been Jack and Lola's doctor for twenty-five years, and Penny had now cared for both of them in this nursing home. She was on the floor every week, and because Lola was mentally sharp, Penny and Lola became close. Lola had a way of opening people's hearts, and all the caregivers would drop by to chat even if she wasn't their patient that day. Penny would take extra time and sit with Lola and talk. They talked about each other's families and things they loved to do.

She was dear to us and would return our calls immediately if we needed her. If she was on the floor when we arrived, we always exchanged hugs and talked about the latest tests or blood work. During those days, she was a comfort that made the journey softer.

At Lola's memorial service, I saw a tearful Penny sitting in the back. Those are the small, unexpected moments that touch your heart, the evidence of more than a partnership but a friend.

Chapter 14

Getting the Bad News

A Diagnosis

Huntington's disease (HD) is a hereditary disease in our family. It is a genetic disorder that causes a progressive breakdown of cells in the brain resulting in cognitive impairment and involuntary movements of face, arms, and legs. Onset of HD is usually late-forties, and life expectancy is fifteen to twenty-five years. Late symptoms can be difficulty swallowing and choking. There is no effective treatment or cure, and each child of a Huntington's patient has a fifty-fifty chance of getting the disease. Terrible odds. It is a cruel disease.

HD has been traced back to my great-grandmother Bliss, born in 1883, and was inherited by three of her four children—my Grandmother Edris Ackerman and her twin brothers, Verle and Merle. They all exhibited symptoms by their late forties, but by then, they were all married and had children. Verle and Merle checked themselves into nursing facilities by fifty years of age. Verle's two sons inherited the disease. Merle's extreme movements made him slide out of a chair or a bed, so his nursing home room had cushioned floors and padded walls so he wouldn't harm himself. My father was named after his Uncle

Verle. He remembers visiting them both in the nursing home. We now know it was Huntington's disease, but it was undiagnosed then. This disease was identified too late for our family to know it was hereditary.

Therefore, my Grandmother Edris Ackerman had four children. My father, Verle, was the oldest child. We all watched Grandma navigate illness as she also had epilepsy. I was with her quite often growing up but never remember having a meaningful conversation. She went through extreme behavioral changes, and my grandfather Ackerman always seemed to find a way to keep her home and manage her illness. Her movements were more subtle, like walking crooked, leaning to the side, head and arms moving back and forth, scrunching her mouth and eyes. She often choked and had difficulty swallowing. She was in a skilled nursing home the last two years.

I just wanted you to get the picture of the impact to our family. When the diagnosis of Huntington's disease was told to my grandmother, everyone expected her adult children to develop HD also. But when all four of them passed their fifties with absolutely no symptoms, we felt sure that all of the family were home free.

In 2005, when my father was eighty, I noticed him rocking back and forth when he was standing. His feet had involuntary movements when he was sitting. I also noticed that his inbox was piling up in his office. He was leaving more office work for my visits, and he was beginning to be confused. I received a call from his brother expressing a real concern about changes in his thinking. They wanted me to do something and felt it may be HD symptoms. I had already noticed but didn't want to believe it. I had to pull my head out of the sand.

This diagnosis could have dynamics for the entire family, especially my brother and me. Dad and I made an appointment with a neurologist that specializes in movement disorders. He had various tests and sent bloodwork for HD genetic testing.

The test results took a few months, but Dad and I had enough talks and observations to know the truth.

At the time, Dad was still driving, attending church, taking care of Mom, and enjoying life. Dad had been healthy and high energy his entire life. This was a real hard pill to swallow because we knew what the future would look like.

Two months later, Dad and I made the long drive back to the doctor's office in downtown Jacksonville. On the way I said, "Dad, we already know what the results will be. Nothing right now in your life is going to change. You will still live your life, go to church, spend time with your family, go to Cracker Barrel, and do everything that you have been doing. We already know that this form of HD is different. It is late-onset. It may be less impactful. You are not your mom. I will be with you every step, and we are going to keep living." A little rah-rah speech.

We went into the doctor's office together and received the bad news that the test was positive for the HD gene. The young doctor had never seen anyone with HD at eighty and was continuing to talk, but my mind went blank. I went numb. The news hit us both like a kick in the stomach, and I was too rattled to ask important questions. We walked in silence to the car, arm in arm. When I turned the car on, I heard a small whimper. My hero was humped over, tears running down his face. "Oh Cathy, what are we going to do?" We both wept.

We sat in the car for a long time, and I let him talk through all his thoughts. His concerns were for everyone else. Dad was worried about Mama and how it would impact her. I just let him talk and cry. He took his glasses off and wiped his eyes with the white hanky from his pocket. He wondered how the rest of the family would deal with the news.

We then turned the conversation to our Lord. It's what we always do. It's the way we live. Dad was thankful for a joy-filled, blessed life. His fifty years of ministry was far beyond what he and Mom ever dreamed. Such a happy life and love together. They still lived every day to the fullest. When I was growing up, my mom often said, "How are you going to carry yourself through this?" She was referring to dignity, strength, and faith. Her voice was in my head now.

I again told him that nothing changed today, to just keep living, enjoying every minute, and that we would do great. We hugged, dried our eyes, and got ready to face the future. At home, I watched my hero get out of the car. No hanky, just a cape. God was by his side just like every other day.

You are never fully prepared and will still go through stages of grief. So it is better to express emotions and work through your thoughts out loud. You will always need support, hope, normalcy, and a strong faith that will maintain the peace and joy in your life.

People will have different approaches to how they navigate through it. Listen, and above all, talk it out along the way. In all cases of difficult news, it is something you go through together. It is sorrowful and tests you in every way, but there is also life to be lived during it all.

So do you ask God, "Why did you let this happen?" Well, God isn't surprised at the test results. God's best plan is still in progress, and you will live it all the way through, and you will get through it. This will be an important part of your life, as important as a career, raising children, and all the many wonderful parts. My dad was still Dad, living out his faith and passing out joy in a different way. This is life.

Being the example for others shows your children how to live with purpose and how to love. Now is the opportunity to demonstrate how to navigate these steps in faith. If you are the daughter or the son, you are demonstrating to your own children how to tenderly walk this path, possibly with you someday. They will learn how to carry themselves through hard times. It's a way of purpose and faith, not fear.

Chapter 15

Come Live with Me

It was a split-second decision that had been a long time coming. They stayed in their home until the last possible moment.

The Time Had Come

"Come live with me, Mom."

"Are you sure?" I felt her following behind me. "You know what you are signing up for, don't you?"

I turned. "What, Mom?"

"You will walk with me."

"Walk where?"

"You'll walk me to heaven." Our eyes locked. "I know. It's okay."

We knew what she was saying.

And it began. My parents would leave the home they loved, their family, church, and lifetime friends in Jacksonville and move with us to Pennsylvania, an unknown house, an unknown place. Never to see home again.

What Contributing Factors Led to This Decision?

For years my schedule included regular visits with my parents. I attended doctor appointments, organized the medication, and did office work. When I drove away, they were happy, in good shape, and waving from the front porch. Those days were over. For the last six months, I felt awful when I drove away and often stayed longer.

Physical Decline

Many factors culminated in the conclusion of living with us. Dad was eighty-five. It had been almost five years since his Huntington's diagnosis, and his physical capabilities had decreased. I remember the day he hesitated to get on an escalator. His balance and coordination wouldn't allow him to step on and hold the rail. He had fallen a few times at home, which made him insecure. At the beginning, I was caught off guard. I had to adjust from the vivacious, capable image of my dad.

Mental Decline

The neurologist noticed mental decline and ordered a battery of memory tests with a psychologist. We met with the psychologist, and she asked a few preliminary questions. I saw the exasperation on his face. She excused me, administered the test, and called me back in. The diagnosis indicated a decline in memory, language, problem-solving, and other thinking skills that affected his ability to perform everyday activities. We had another tough ride home because this test confirmed our concerns.

Loss of Independence

Our next appointment with the neurologist took us by surprise. He had received the memory test results and concluded that Dad was no longer capable of driving. His reflexes and his thinking skills were diminished enough to put him at risk of an accident. I thanked the doctor as we left. Dad did not.

This ride home was a bit more testy than sorrowful. We

discussed that he needed to turn over the keys, and he said it was impossible to live without driving. I told him that the diagnosis was now officially in his health record, and he could be held liable if there was an accident, even if he was not at fault. He said that he had to think about it. He is my dad. I did not argue.

Two weeks later, he quit driving on his own. The next time I came, we serviced the car and sold it to a couple in the church.

Ability to Cope

So here were two people with declining physical and mental abilities. Mom didn't recognize his mental decline and had the same expectations of him. Dad had lost the ability to deal with her dementia and lack of ability to reason. He was constantly frustrated with her, which was a totally new wrinkle. Patience had declined in them both.

Dad called me on the phone one afternoon. He was on the front porch, sitting in a rocking chair, crying. It was all too much. Even with home care, family, and friends, he was at the end. We had discussed moving in with me on several occasions. Mom was ready. Dad had not been, until today.

Unified Decision

Clayton and I talked at home that night and discussed the dynamics of the move. I was scheduled to go to Jacksonville, and he joined me. When Clayton and Dad took their usual walk together, Clayton said, "I think you need to come live with us. Two reasons. First, you both are at the place you need care. Second, I want my wife back."

They both chuckled. I was so fortunate that they had such a sweet love for each other. Dad knew it was time and agreed.

A Thoughtful Transition

I was warned that moving a senior or a person with dementia was very traumatic. My goal was to make their part of the house feel familiar. I had already had furniture which included an early-American four-poster bed that Mom loved and a dresser. I packed their bedspread and curtains from their room and brought Dad's desk, file cabinets, and burgundy curtains from his office. I knew that I could make it feel like home for them.

I went to Jacksonville and boxed up just the items that would go to Pennsylvania. A moving truck came and took some boxes, clothes, the curtains, the bedspread, and Dad's office to my house in Pennsylvania.

The moving truck met me in Pennsylvania a few days later. I unpacked their clothes and set up their bedroom suite and living room with Dad's office. I also bought a comfy recliner for the bedroom. It felt and looked like their own home.

Clayton and I went back to Florida to get my parents. The whole family joined us at the airport for a sendoff. My dad's brothers and their families had all stepped up and given them love and attention for years. They were sorry to see them go but relieved that they were being cared for. Dad and Mom were excited about the flight and seeing their new home. The move was a sacrifice for the whole family, but a welcomed one.

A New Beginning

As the four of us pulled down the long drive of our new home, a family of deer were standing under the trees. You can't make this up. It was a peaceful setting for Lucille. This older home had a cozy kitchen looking over the backyard and a den with a large stone fireplace. Mom and Dad walked into their bedroom suite and living quarters. Dad was delighted to see his desk and computer all set up and the files in place, and Mom couldn't believe she had her own bedspread and curtains. Everything was in the drawers and closet, and her jewelry box was on the dresser, just like home. The bathroom had her own towels, rugs, and the same curtain in the window. Even though her furniture wasn't there, the décor was complete with personal pictures on the walls. It was home.

Clayton and I will never forget those first moments. They walked out of their new bedroom and Mom said, "You did this for us?" They both had tears in their eyes and that made it worth it.

Later that day, Mom called for help. I said, "Dad, you've been on duty for years. I will take over from here. This is what the move is all about."

He put both hands on his face and said, "Ah, bless you." He was done carrying the load. We installed a button in their bedroom and bathroom. It rang a remote doorbell in the hall upstairs. Day or night, I answered the bell, and Dad didn't move a muscle. The move improved Dad's quality of life and gave Mom her Cathy time. Clayton and I had a new mission together.

Developing a Routine

Knowing my parents would miss their friends and family and experience grief, I immediately tried to develop a familiar routine but also created new activities in their day. We started the morning with the usual oatmeal and toast but ate on the back deck overlooking the trees. They loved it. I set up a speaker and created a playlist of their favorite music while they ate. We sat there for an hour and talked and enjoyed being outside. It was summer and beautiful weather.

Dad spent the next few hours at his desk and computer, watching television while I helped Mom shower and dress. After she dressed, she picked out jewelry, a scarf, and put on her makeup. Then I curled her hair with a curling iron. Anyway, she was happy, Dad was happy, mission accomplished.

I discovered that Dad was easily content in his office and living room, but Mom wanted something to do. *Piddle around*, she called it. So I saved little things for her to do each day. Her neuropathy had caused damage to her hand and arm, so I had to design tasks that were suited to one hand. I determined that she could help make the bed and straighten up her bathroom and bedroom, so I got her started and left her to finish. It took her hours to do things, which filled up her day.

Slowly several other activities filled her day. Mom could fold the napkins and set the table and put away clothes from the dryer. I bought a feather duster. She set items aside, dusted, and rearranged the shelf. She also liked to organize her clothes in her closet. She would sit and talk while I cooked. A large box of photographs interested her, taking long looks, then putting them in stacks. She would discuss stories about the person or place. I determined what movies interested her and put one on in the afternoon. Thus, plenty of piddling activities.

Dad was content as could be. Breakfast and lunch lasted hours. After sixty years of marriage, they still could spend hours talking. Each morning he walked the long driveway for the paper and spent a few hours combing through it. Then he would be at his desk corresponding with Facebook friends. After lunch he sat on the porch watching the activity of the neighborhood.

Several afternoons we would take a long drive. They loved the rolling hills of Pennsylvania and seeing Amish farms. When winter came, the fireplace and snowfall were a real treat for them. The kitchen table had a beautiful view of the back yard. I was surprised that they loved bundling up to go out.

Hope for a Future

Hope and a future, something to look forward to. When a career is done, the purpose for living often goes with it. What's a reason to get up today? Anxiety, depression, and increased pain occur when there is no hope, no future.

Short- and long-term events were planned and talked about for weeks. An afternoon walk, sitting on the porch, or a movie created an anchor for each day. Our weekly routine included a Friday lunch at Cracker Barrel or an afternoon at the mall. A future event, like Thanksgiving or a visiting relative, brought hours of anticipation.

As their physical and mental capabilities diminished, their world became smaller. So the phone calls and visits from friends and family kept them interested in the outside world. We set a calendar for family birthdays so they could call or send a card. Something to look forward to or talk about and plan. A future.

Home Care Assistance

After a few months of establishing a routine, I realized that a caregiver from nine until one would allow me to run errands and identify a person that could stay for a few days when we took a trip. A local agency found a caregiver that was the perfect fit. Maryann became a great friend and caregiver to Mom. She helped her shower, dress, threw in some laundry, and made lunch. She lived alone, was in her mid-fifties, and had several children and grandchildren in the area. She was a tireless worker, very engaging with us, and rolled with the punches.

Not Always Rosy

A change in medication often caused agitation. Dementia caused ups and downs in Mom's emotions. A big frustration between her and Dad was the cat. Yes, the cat. Clayton is not a cat enthusiast. Remember, everyone must sacrifice. I'll just leave it there. But Mom came and so did the cat. Luckily, it stayed under things and out of sight.

The frustration was that Mom wanted the cat to be warm at night. Everyone would be all nestled in bed asleep, and the sweet little cat would jump up and run across the bed and wake them.

The cat was fine, but Mom thought it wanted to be in bed, covered up. We all know that you can't make a cat do anything. But Mom had it in her sweet head that she had to find the cat in the middle of the night. She was up and all over the place at two a.m. Dad couldn't reason with her, so he pushed the button, and I came down.

I learned to get on her side of the struggle and look for the sweet little bundle of fur in the middle of the night. I had to keep Dad from talking, the cat from running, and Mom from crawling around looking under furniture. It was a zoo. I was exhausted but had to hold it together; there was no time to fall apart now. If it hadn't been in the middle of the night, it would have been amusing.

Getting to Know You

After a lifetime with your parents, you would assume that you know everything there is to know about them. But the greatest outcome of this entire journey was the stories that I never knew about them.

When my dad was seven years old, a teenage girl, Geraldine, from the Methodist church in town started a children's Bible class. She walked from farm to farm inviting the kids to come on Sunday. Dad went alone for several years, his first experience with anything spiritual or religious.

A few years later, the whole family began attending, but his dad wanted to look for a church that taught the Bible. He heard about a new church in the area, and their family visited on Sunday. The pastor was Elbert Bowers, and he had a daughter, Lucille. They were eleven years old when they met, Verle and Lucille. My parents began dating when they were sixteen, married when they were nineteen.

At seven years old, when Geraldine knocked on the door, Dad gave his life to the Lord. The journey of faith included over fifty years of ministry. When Dad was sixty, he watched thousands of people streaming into the sanctuary. He thought, "Lord, look what you've done!" He remembered the seven-year-old farm boy and thought about God's miracle hand on his life.

They told me sweet stories of love and faith during our meals together, often with tears.

This Is My Life

Growing up, I thought about life, never envisioning this part of the journey. But now I know that this was my greatest joy. I felt it was God's personal call on my life to care for these two servants. I was witness to their lives of dedication to Him and was privileged to walk them to heaven. I saw them live in faith and die in faith.

Chapter 16

Assisted Living, Nursing Home, Memory Care

Caring for my parents at home was the plan, but as Huntington's disease set in for my dad, I realized that he needed more than I could provide. Discouraged, I talked to a friend that just lost his wife after years of care. He said, "At some point you should just be his daughter, not his caregiver." After those words, I gave myself permission to seek the options of care.

No Judgment Here

Give yourself permission to consider the whole picture, and you'll realize that while the professionals give physical and medical care, you'll provide the comfort and love. That's what's important.

You cannot make every moment happy or pain-free, but you can make it better. I was in the weeds, trying to make everything perfect. Every pain relieved, every smudge wiped, every shirt wrinkle-free, every caregiver kind, every need met, no unhappiness or loneliness. Unrealistic.

My family and friends stated the obvious. My parents' lives were better because of me. Consider what is best for them and for you too. Not perfection, just the best you can do today. There is no right, wrong, or perfect answer.

The Decision for a Senior Community

What determining factors drive the decision? Many parents make their own move to a senior living community so their health needs will automatically trigger the level of care within that facility as they age.

Several years ago, my dad's sister Joanne moved into independent living with her husband Lloyd. The house and yard were too much work, so they downsized to a two-bedroom villa with a garage in a senior community. They were active and enjoyed the community. When Uncle Lloyd went to heaven, Aunt Joanne moved to assisted living in the main building. She eats meals in the dining room with friends and is involved in activities during the day. Her two daughters live nearby, so Joanne spends time with them, but she loves living life at her own pace, socializing when she wants to or quilting in her room. She's ninety-two.

Levels of Care

Independent Living: An apartment or villa with a full kitchen, living room, bedrooms, and parking. In our case, they provided weekly housekeeping, a restaurant with a meal plan, and activities.

Assisted Living: An apartment with a refrigerator and included assistance as needed with bathing, dressing, housekeeping, and medication. An attending nurse is designated for the facility; daily activities and meals are provided.

Memory Care: A single room and bathroom with full-time caregiving for bathing, dressing, hygiene, housekeeping, medication, meals, and activities. Nursing staff is available.

Nursing Home: A skilled nursing facility with a room for one or two occupants. Meals, medications, and total nursing provided, in addition to physical or occupational therapy, some activities, like a hospital with twenty-four-hour nursing care.

When Life Changes

It was the last day Dad would ever spend in our house. We just didn't know it. Friday was our day out, and of course we went to Cracker Barrel for lunch, then did a little shopping. It was a good day, and after enjoying dinner, we all turned in for the evening. At two a.m., Clayton and I heard a crash and found him on the floor in his bathroom. He had forgotten his walker by the bed.

He was yelling, "Oh! Oh! It hurts, it hurts so bad. What have I done, Cathy?" I didn't move him, just retrieved a pillow and covered him with a blanket. I helped him to breathe long slow breaths and calm himself while Clayton called 911 and directed the medics.

I grabbed the emergency envelope by the front door. Inside, the health list included all the things that the medics needed to know. I gave them a copy and made sure that there was another for the hospital, along with his living will. I always had his insurance and ID in my wallet.

They lifted him onto the gurney as he cried out loud. I would have traded places in a heartbeat. My sweet daddy was so confused and in pain. I packed a small bag for him, and we followed the ambulance.

As soon as the doctor stepped in the room, I said, "Before we get started, what can you do for the immediate pain?" He looked at Dad's few medications, asked another question, and sent the nurse for a shot. When Dad's pain eased and he rested, then the doctor continued.

On Sunday morning he had surgery for a broken hip. His bones were strong, and they were confident that he would recover. That was not the case. True, his bones were strong, and the hip surgery was a success, but the Huntington's disease, his balance, and mental decline combined to defeat every effort to get him up and walking.

After Dad's hip surgery, a rehab facility followed. When he stood, his legs gave out without warning. He couldn't comb his hair, brush his teeth, shower, dress, or toilet. He needed assistance transferring from the bed to his wheelchair. Mental confusion impacted his ability to help.

It was shocking how, after his fall, his mental and physical capacity never recovered. You are always told that a fall for the elderly is often the beginning of the end. That is the truth.

The Rehab Facility

The rehab facility after Dad's surgery was a nightmare. They were short staffed. Dad was taken to the dining hall with no shoes and hair uncombed, and he had no assistance at the table. He couldn't open a carton of milk, so he had no drink.

The physical therapists were determined to get him walking. I had to explain that Huntington's disease hampered the control of his arms and legs. He wasn't mentally able to understand their instructions, and he was frustrated. They were impatient with him, and Dad yelled at them to stop it. He had never raised his voice. He was frightened.

Clayton and I went to the director of the facility, and she apologized for staff shortages. We walked back on his floor, and Dad was in a wheelchair beside the nurse station asking for his daughter. The nurse said, "Just go back to your room."

He couldn't have even found his room. I thought Clayton was going to jump over the desk. Instead, he said, "That's it." We searched for another option.

That experience sent up red flags of how important family oversight is when a loved one is under anyone else's care. Elder neglect and abuse in facilities is more common that I thought. Do you know the saying, "Never EXpect what you don't

INspect"? That's why family needs to visit at random hours, check the processes for cleanliness, for nourishing food, for hiring practices, and become a fixture in that place. Check your loved one for bruises, bedsores, and clean hygiene practices. Talk with the other patients' family members, have an outside PA or doctor visit each month, and check the medication process. Watch, ask, listen.

The Crossroad of Care

We were ready to bundle Dad up and take him home. But what were his needs now? And what was our capability? A crossroad.

Physical Requirements: No mobility demanded a higher level of care. Physically, I was incapable of lifting or transferring him, and Clayton had a bad back. Dad couldn't mentally or physically assist me, and the two of us slid to the ground a few times. It was a wakeup call.

A Case of Gender: Dad was not comfortable with his daughter toileting, dressing, and showering him. Also, showering him now required two people. This was another piece to the puzzle and reaffirmed that I should be his daughter, not his caregiver.

Mental Decline: Dad's mental decline threatened his physical safety. He didn't remember hip surgery, Huntington's disease, or falling. He had walked his whole life, so he stood up to walk instinctively, and no amount of reminding made any difference. I feared another fall and surgery.

Future Outlook: The characteristics of HD's progressive mental and physical decline and finally swallowing and choking would make skilled nursing inevitable. I knew what was ahead.

Social Needs: Dad was still alert enough to be social. He was engaging, thankful, and welcoming. Having interactions and activities to fill his days would be enriching for him.

Comparative Cost: Knowing the need for 24/7 care, we did the math for day and night care and compared it to nursing care.

One caregiver was just as expensive as nursing care, and I would always have to be available as a second person.

Finances often dictate the care, and as I said before, I've seen adult children provide quality care for their loved one with no financial resources, and I've watched families with financial advantages provide assisted living but emotionally neglect their moms and dads. Money is just a tool for options, but loving is the real quality that can't be bought.

The Perfect Solution for Care

Clayton's brother Brian told me about a beautiful senior community. He encouraged me to at least ask them for advice. I knew that independent or assisted living was not enough and felt like a nursing home was not a fit either. We met with Lisa, the director of admissions, and discussed what was needed. Lisa said, "Have you thought about memory care?" I immediately cringed at the thought.

Lisa said, "Let me show you around our community, and we will stop in the memory care." We entered the wing known as Ensemble. It was peaceful and well-staffed with only twenty-four residents. In the living room, several residents and caregivers sat in winged-back chairs watching TVs. One side of an activity room offered bingo, and on the other side, residents were sitting in a circle laughing and kicking a ball. The caregivers and residents were enjoying themselves.

We met the activity director, who was handing out the afternoon snack to several men sitting on the back porch. A caregiver was engaging them in conversation. The dining room was set for dinner, complete with tablecloths and china. It was lovely, peaceful, and clean.

The residents and caregivers were busy all day. They told us that musicians were scheduled to sing oldies, and a man regularly brought his dog to entertain. There were decorations for

Christmas, and a holiday party was planned for residents and their families.

So, at this point, it would seem like an easy decision, but as Lisa and Clayton talked about the next steps, I was numb. I was heartbroken. How could I do this to my sweet dad? What would Mom think? What did the Lord want me to do?

The next day, two nurses from memory care came to assess if Dad's physical and mental level was a fit. They were delightful, and Dad loved them right away. His face lit up as they engaged together. We told Dad that he needed further rehab, and he was grateful to leave the current rehab. Finally, I had great peace.

The Move to Memory Care

Move-in day was December 1. Each resident had to provide furniture for their bedroom. His bed, chest of drawers, TV, recliner, nightstand, and lamps were delivered. Familiar things.

He had his own bedspread along with the matching pillow shams. His sister had quilted him a blanket, and it was draped over his recliner. The picture of his church hung on the wall, and two memory albums sat on a small table.

All his sports shirts, navy pants, and sweaters were neatly hanging in the closet. The toiletries were in the bathroom, and his pajamas, T-shirts, and socks were folded in his drawer. It was all I could do.

The activity director for memory care, the head nurse, and the caregiver met us as we arrived. They asked him what he liked to eat and what he liked to do. They were getting the feel of his communication skills. He was happy to be somewhere better than the rehab. He was not aware this was memory care, just another rehab to continue getting better from his fall.

They pushed him into the activity room where all the residents were singing and doing motions with their arms. He joined in, keeping an eye on me in the back. At supper, he sat with three other men at the table and began eating, so I slipped out, a mixture of happy and sad.

Setting Expectations for His Care

Linda was his caregiver. Soft spoken and kind. She talked with him as she cared for him. She let him do as much as he could, encouraging him.

Monday through Thursday, Linda shaved him, combed his hair, and dressed him. The other three days a week were often different caregivers to fill in Friday and the weekend. No shave, no T-shirt, shirt untucked, no sweater. When I arrived, I would find his caregiver and sweetly ask her to shave him. While we were in the room, I would pull out the T-shirt and the sweater, and we would tuck in the shirt.

I was very kind and appreciative but not shy to get it right. The caregivers learned how to care for him. I had been asked by both of my parents to pay attention to their hygiene and appearance as they aged. I had promised.

Dad always looked clean and neat. This facility did a good job hiring and training, and the head nurse, activity director, and his caregivers were eager to please.

Scheduling My Visits

I learned to vary my visit schedule when Lola was in skilled nursing. When I visited her the same time in the afternoon, if I didn't make it or was late, she was anxious and in her wheelchair at the elevator door waiting for me. I changed my ways quickly. When I varied my visiting times—early morning, or afternoon, or evening—she was not anxious. So I did the same with my dad. He did ask for me every day, and they would assure him I would be there.

Varying the times of my visits allowed me to observe different activities and caregivers during the day. After breakfast, the residents sat in the living room and exercised with the activity director. I would pull a chair next to Dad and join in. Later in the morning, they would sit outside in the garden or on the porch and listen to music. After lunch, most of the residents would go to their rooms for a nap or play bingo in the activity room.

Every time I came, we went to his room, and he stretched out in his recliner. His back and legs needed it. Most of the time we watched TV, or sometimes we would call a sibling and let them talk to him. I straightened his closet and drawers and made a list of items he needed. I cut and cleaned his nails, trimmed unwanted hairs, and put lotion on his hands. We often looked at the pictures in the memory album. He loved the attention, and we would talk. Kind of.

When Clayton visited, he took Dad out in the garden, and they talked and sang together. In fact, Dad's memory of hymns was intact, and he still knew how to pray. When he saw Clayton come in, he would lift his arms and say, "There's my best friend." Everyone knew about Clayton. He noticed things about my dad that I didn't and brought balance to his care.

Exit strategy. Dad would usually fret and ask where I was going, how far it was, when I would be back, and could he come with me. So I usually left at snack time or mealtime. He loved to eat, and he focused right away on the task at hand. I slipped out when they moved him to his table.

They Called Him Pastor

When Dad arrived at memory care, the nurse asked, "What do you want us to call you?"

"I'm Pastor."

The answer surprised me, but not really. Pastor was what thousands of people called him.

The first day at memory care, he assigned himself as a greeter. When visitors or facility staff walked through, he would say, "Hello!" or "How are you?" Everyone stopped, talked to him, and shook his hand. It was fun to watch how they greeted him. "Hello, Pastor."

His Final Pulpit

I occasionally wondered why God allowed Dad to go through this, and what the purpose of this time was. Shame on me. God was still using him in people's lives. He was still a minister, caring for those around him.

The caregivers would tell us that he prayed with them. Their hearts were touched. One Sunday afternoon, a young caregiver knelt beside him and said, "My daughter and I went to church today, Pastor." Then she told us that she and Dad had a talk, and he said her daughter needed to learn about God. She said, "I knew he was right."

Within a year, his persona dimmed, but people would seek him out and spend a minute checking on Pastor. He always brightened up and said, "I'm fine. You okay?" His vocabulary eventually decreased to a few phrases. "God bless you. Thank you. You okay? Praying for you." It was evident that even as his mind dimmed, God was close.

The head nurse said how dear Dad was. I said, "I wish you had known Dad when his mind was strong."

She said, "Oh, this is good enough for me."

I have sweet memories of this place. It was a daily home for two years. I loved the residents that were there and the other family members spent time with Dad, and I did the same with their loved one. And the caregivers loved my dad like he was their grandfather. You can't put words to it. They cared for me too. It was a special place with special people.

Chapter 17

Dying Well

To What End?

Quality of life is about comfort instead of suffering. It's about enhancing the experience of life. When you face an end-of-life decision for your spouse, parent, or yourself, it's usually based on timing, and that's why the health surrogate and living will documents are important for everyone at any age.

Remember, the medications and machines can keep someone alive for months and years, so it's not a matter of keeping them alive as much as to what end? All four of our parents could have been kept alive. The machines exist and the treatments could go on and on, but to what end? They were already in deteriorating health when a critical condition occurred.

I know it's an uncommon thought to die well. But don't we all want our inevitable experience to be done with thought and care? When do we let nature take its course? When do we let medicine step in and lengthen life?

Jack—Loving Enough to Let Him Go

This dear man in our life, crusty and lively, was an anchor that developed character into the lives of his sons for over forty years. He experienced unconditional love and learned to love back. He was tough and tender.

His last year of life was a challenge. In the nursing home, he was disoriented and hard to control. The complication of being an amputee made the daily routine not routine at all, but Lola was relentless in her care.

Jack's poor circulation caused an infection in his other leg. A hospitalization revealed that another amputation was necessary to save his life. So, here was the question. To what end? The surgery itself would cause more suffering, and the outcome from the surgery would be another decrease in quality of life. Lola chose to let nature take its course and use medicine to provide comfort care instead of treatment.

It was the right decision to call in hospice. Jack didn't know. He didn't fret, just rested. We turned our attention to the process of Jack dying well. Loving him, comforting him. Peacefully.

Lola—She Did It Her Way

You can tell my love for Lola. Her name brings a smile, even today. She always knew what she wanted and orchestrated life wherever she was. Her life success depended on her alone, and her choices were honored even at this point.

Lola's great-grandchildren brought life into her world during her nursing home stay. She kept candy or dollar bills in her nightstand, and when the little ones came in, she would get a treat for them. One day, her great-granddaughter came hopping in saying, "Grandma, I'll help you get the treat for me," as she ran to the nightstand and retrieved a dollar bill.

Lola's last month in the nursing home, her vitals began to

fail, and she physically gave way. Appetite disappeared, breathing shallowed, and the brightness in her eyes dimmed as her attempts to communicate faded. Finally, she was hospitalized for pneumonia, but she didn't respond to the medication. There were no drastic decisions to be made. It was time to call hospice.

Lucille—Brave Decision

On a December Sunday morning Dad, Mom, and I attended church and spent a quiet day together. Clayton was out of town. That night, Mom rang the bell from her bedroom. She was in pain, so I followed the steps of diagnosis and attempted the usual remedies.

Remember, she would do anything to avoid the hospital. However, the pain was so intense she wanted to go to the hospital, a clue that this was serious. I called our caregiver to stay with Dad, and I called Clayton. I picked up her health list and IDs and assisted her into the car.

Regrets—I Had A Few

Of all the decisions made for my parents, there is one that stayed with me, one that I regret. After several tests, Mom was diagnosed with a bowel blockage, so the initial treatment required tubes down her nose into her stomach. As the ER doc and nurse began, she was crying and fighting them saying, "No, stop." It went on for fifteen minutes. They were forcing, she was yelling.

I was so upset, and I don't know why I didn't stop them and simply talk to her. If I had listened, it could have saved her days of suffering. But I thought the situation would be remedied and life would go on, but this time she was done. I just didn't realize it was Mom's *to what end* decision.

The next morning, the nurse told me that Mom pulled the tubes out of her nose again. The hospital continued testing, taking blood samples, prodding, poking, and doing their best to diagnose and treat. She was in misery. The nurse came in with tubes again. Mom said, "No."

So, I sat on her bed to explain. She said, "No more tubes, no more needles, no more tests." Her blue eyes gave me "The Look" as she pointed her finger. The message was, "Got it?" But as her daughter, I was trying to grasp the outcome of her request. I had always fought for life and to find a solution, so what now?

Later, a surgeon arrived announcing that surgery was needed, and she said, "No surgery." So for the surgeon's benefit, I said, "Mom, if you don't allow the surgery, you probably won't make it." Then she said in a clear, adamant tone, "Either God will heal me or take me home." Decision made. Where did this clarity of mind come from?

This was Mom's *to what end* conclusion. She didn't want to go through surgery and back to the everyday pain and deteriorating health. There was no real recovery and quality of life that she desired. She was done, after a lifetime of migraines, shots, surgeries, hospitals, and daily pain, she had suffered enough. Yes, she packed in a lot of living during her eighty-nine years, but now her eyes were in a different direction, heaven bound.

The next few days, I became her advocate for death. I don't know a more palatable way of stating it. We just let nature take its course. She had made the call, but still the surgeon, the nurse, her primary physician, and hospice all made the attempt to challenge her decision. The medical team kept questioning as she said, "Please no." It was another moment to roll up my sleeves, put my hair behind my ears, and transition everyone's thinking from treatment to comfort care. Clayton, Dad, and I had meetings to plan the transfer to hospice.

It took another day before the medical team changed gears, but I helped Mom settle into a restful peace. I brought in music as she lay quietly. Doug Oldham sang, "The Longer I Serve Him, The Sweeter He Grows." I smiled as I saw her foot below the sheet keeping time. As I sat beside her, she reached for my wrist and whispered, "That's my girl." I recalled our conversation years before and knew this was our *walk me to heaven* time. She was taken to a hospice facility near the hospital.

Verle—Dad and Pastor

Dad's days in memory care fell into a comfortable routine. The caregivers were engaging, and the care was far better than I could have hoped. Besides the occasional fall, Dad never had an ache or pain, slept like a baby, and cleaned his plate. He was content most of the time, and Clayton often reminded me that I can't make him happy every single minute, but I tried.

Dad was not sure where he was exactly, but he always knew when I walked through the door. His face lit up like it had since I was born, one of his greatest gifts to me. We enjoyed just being.

About nine months before he went to heaven, he began developing recurring infections. He would get a high fever that increased the Huntington's disease symptoms. He became unable to swallow, sit up, or control his arms and legs. Several hospitalizations resulted because the only effective treatment was IV antibiotics.

The physician's assistant who visited him in memory care knew that the infections were taking a toll on him. Every time he went to the hospital and treatment, I asked myself why I was putting him through such misery. His Huntington's disease was worsening with choking, falling, disorientation, and anxiety. We couldn't get the medications right to get him comfortable.

So I discussed with the PA, the nurse at memory care, and the family about his condition. Dad and I had often discussed how the Huntington's symptoms in the end were so distressful. It was what he dreaded most about the disease.

Clayton and I, the PA, and the memory care nurse decided there were to be no more trips to the hospital. The next time he became ill, hospice came to care for him. I often think about that decision. I could have continued the rounds of hospitalizations until he deteriorated from HD, but I didn't want that for him. Suffering was what I wanted to avoid. I let God choose the timing by letting nature take its course. A life of suffering versus heaven. I chose heaven. It was time for hospice.

Several weeks before, a gentleman down the hall died. When his wife passed by, Dad had said, "I'm praying for you." Dad didn't even know about her husband, but God did. Later, she told Clayton and me how much Dad had comforted her. There was one last ministry moment for Pastor.

The sobering night my father went to heaven, Clayton and I thought about each of our dear parents. Being an orphan was a strange sensation that we weren't prepared to experience. Without parents, who would provide that deep level of love? Who else so closely witnessed our life? Who would advise us with unselfish insight? Where was our soft place to fall now? We both felt the sudden aloneness. Together.

Having no parents also means, that in the grand scheme of generations, it pushes us up a level. We are next in line. What? That, in itself, puts us right up there as old. Instead of being the kids taking care of the parents, we are them now. It has changed how we think about ourselves, and I don't like it at all.

Chapter 18

Hospice Care

From Treatment to Comfort Care

Sarah Young's April 14 devotional in *Jesus Calling* says, "Heaven is both present and future. As you walk along your life-path holding His hand, you are already in touch with the essence of heaven – *Nearness to Me*. At the end of your life-path is an 'Entrance to Heaven.' I am preparing you each step of the way."

Hospice's Family Support

Hospice is a word that is often whispered. Just the word hospice unnerves a family often to tears. It correlates with dying—an uncharted, uncomfortable, emotional event.

So what does hospice bring to the table? For the family, hospice skillfully turns a distressful event into meaningful moments. These experienced doctors and nurses care for dying loved ones and their families every day.

The hospice doctors will evaluate the loved one and become acquainted with the family. They learn about the family faith, expectations, and concerns, and ask if a family member is on the way. They determine the comfort level of the family at the moment of death. The team gets an understanding of how to communicate the phases and timeframe.

The Hospice Team

Hospice takes over medical care and makes the transition from cure to comfort care. Hospice not only provides physical comfort but also emotional and spiritual care. The team consists of a chaplain, a nurse, a psychologist, and a physician. Each team member is sensitive and experienced for every scenario. The nurse knows the nuances of comfort—nausea, pain, fever, and labored breathing; the chaplain draws close with assurance and comfort; the psychologist reads the signs of anxiety and grief. They slip in and out during the day and night. Their presence is attentive, comforting, and provides subtle hints about what to anticipate next.

Hospice at Home

Hospice is not limited to a hospital. If a loved one is being cared for at home, hospice will send a nurse for an evaluation, determine the needs of the individual and the family, then set up a schedule of regular visits. The hospice visits increase as the loved one declines, but more care is required by the family from administering medications to monitoring changes. There is more responsibility on the family.

Hospice in a Nursing Home

When you have hospice in assisted living, a nursing home, or memory care, hospice has a relationship with most senior care facilities. They have teams of nurses that evaluate and care for senior citizens when they begin their physical decline and are called in by a physician. They will work in coordination with the director of nursing, the physician, and the family to provide rest and maintain constant comfort for a loved one.

The nursing home had taken care of Jack for over a year, and Lola was there every day. Jack constantly asked to go home, and she didn't tell him no. Instead, she told him that he needed to get better first. He became cooperative and peaceful.

After the transition from treatment to comfort care, Jack's caregivers gave him special attention and spent extra time with him. Over the next few days, family members sat with him and watched over Lola as she lovingly comforted.

The hospice team provided a chaplain to talk and pray with him and the family. As the nursing visits increased, she let the family know that the time was near. He fell into a restful sleep as the family held his hands, he took a deep breath, then no more.

Jack didn't know much about heaven. He was older when he began praying and learning about God. Clayton and I imagine that when he opened his eyes in heaven, he said, "Wow, I had no idea."

Hospice in the Hospital

Many hospitals have a designated hospice wing of specialized nursing and care who coordinate with the physician. It offers a quiet, peaceful setting without the need to transport to a facility or home. Hospice will provide continuity of care for your loved one and your family. There is a big difference between a nurse and a hospice nurse.

At the hospital, the nurses settled Lola in a quiet room near the end of the hall. She had been in the hospital for days, becoming weaker. The nurse was not as attentive as Jack's nursing home team had been.

Lola occasionally opened her eyes and mouthed a word to Brian and Clayton as they held her hand and whispered to her. The grandchildren each came and gave her love. She was aware of each one.

The last day, Lola still had oxygen assistance, and her sons asked the nurse why. She had labored breathing for hours. The nurse removed the oxygen, and Lola opened her eyes to look at the family. A moment later, as she eased into a quiet rest, Lola slipped into heaven.

A Hospice Facility

Stand-alone hospice facilities are available in many communities. Often a hospital will transport a patient to a hospice facility for specialized care. The trained staff caters to every need of the patient around the clock. They provide privacy and an environment to support the patient and the family in a cohesive way.

Stephen, the hospice nurse, met Mom at the entrance as the medics rolled her in. He held her hand and leaned close to her face as they walked. "How are you feeling, Lucille? I'm Stephen, your nurse, and I am going to take good care of you." He did.

Mom's room looked like a bedroom with lamps, drapes, a couch, and comfortable chairs. I had composed myself but felt exhausted as I eased onto the couch watching him tuck her in. He looked my way, and I told him I was her daughter. He said, "Let me get her settled, and we'll talk, honey." He "honeyed" me and "babied" mom. We both needed it.

"You miserable, Lucille, dear?"

"Pretty much."

"I'll take care of that right away." Stephen started an IV and began the comfort care.

Her forehead eased as her eyes closed.

"That's better, baby?"

His charm amused her and caused a slight smile. "Yes, better."

A few hours later, Clayton brought Dad into the room and moved a chair by the bed. Dad, as a pastor, had entered the scene of a grieving family hundreds of times. He knew just what to say, how to pray, and how to comfort them. Now he sat by his bride of sixty-eight years and didn't speak. She opened her eyes the final time as he patted her arm. Nothing else needed to be said. It had all been lived out.

As Mom settled into rest and peace, her Savior took her by the hand.

We held each other and prayed, thanking God for blessing us with Lucille and for His tender mercy. We sang, "What a day that will be when my Jesus I shall see…"

Hospice in Memory Care

One Wednesday morning, the nurse from memory care called. Dad had a fever and infection. It had been several weeks since the last infection, and I had hoped the cycle would break. The PA placed the call to hospice.

I got in the car at home wondering what was ahead and not wanting it to be happening now. But it was. Was I ready for this? I took a deep breath.

Dad was hot with fever and coughing. Fever always made the HD movements worse, and he was disoriented. The memory care nurse was in his room taking his temperature. I immediately got cool washcloths for his forehead and another for his neck and began wiping his face. He opened his eyes and said, "Cathy."

"I'm here getting you cooled off."

"Good." He closed his eyes. They agreed to treat the fever as part of making him comfortable.

On Friday, Dad opened his eyes when I talked to him. I stroked his forehead and said, "Hey Dad, how are you feeling?"

"Real good."

We all chuckled, and I said, "Well, that's him. Always the optimist."

That evening at 9:30 p.m., Dad was ushered into heaven to

see the Savior he loved and served his entire life. I'm sure Mom was impatiently waiting. "What took you so long, Verle?"

Psalm 116:15 says, "Precious in the sight of the Lord is the death of his saints" (ESV).

It's a homecoming!

Chapter 19

Celebration of Life

I knew Dad's funeral would be well attended, and I felt pressure to get it right. Anticipating this day, I had conversations with Alan Pue and Guy Melton who grew up in my dad's ministry. They are both excellent speakers, and they committed to be there when the time came.

Growing up, Alan lived a few blocks from my family. His mother was raising him alone and enrolled him in the Christian school at our church. He wanted nothing to do with a Christian school, so he decided to get expelled and succeeded. Dad went to the principal, pled his case, and took responsibility for him. From Alan's version of the story, Dad showed up at his door and said, "You are too valuable. I will not let you go. From this point on, you are mine." Mom and Dad both invested in him and loved him like a son. He was at my house as much as his own. Today he has written several books on Christian education (*Rethinking Discipleship*, *Rethinking Sustainability*, *Rethinking Strategic Planning*) and is a popular consultant and convention speaker for the Christian school movement. And yes, he's Dr. Alan Pue now.

As a child, Guy and his family rode the church bus to Sunday school. The church became his second home along with the Christian school. Dad ministered to his family during some tough times and saw something special in Guy as a young man. He married his high-school sweetheart, and after graduating from Bible college, returned to the church as an associate pastor. Dad's method of apprenticeship was teaching everything from the ground up, so Guy touched every area of ministry and succeeded at every challenge. Rev. Guy Melton has now been in ministry for over forty years and is the senior and founding pastor of Oasis Church of South Florida, a large, multi-ethnic congregation representing almost ninety countries.

They captured the heart of Dad's life and ministry, and it was meaningful for them to share their personal stories. Alan and Guy, along with many others, are ministering in the same way, and I realized that Dad's ministry was still going.

Each parent's funeral involved friends sharing sweet stories, family reading the eulogy, a poem or a song, and the minister giving a celebration of their life. Memorial services put life into perspective and remind us that God provides eternal life and hope.

The Preplanning Gift

Clayton and I felt so relieved that arrangements were paid and completed. It eliminated a long list of tasks when we were exhausted and emotional from the week. Remember, we just left a parent's death bed, our hearts were trying to cope with what just happened, yet there were still decisions to be made.

Funeral Home Responsibilities

1. Assign a coordinator and provide a checklist to guide you through the process.
2. Submit the obituary to the local paper and a

hometown paper if needed. Include it on their website. Do it first thing.
3. Assist in ordering death certificates and notifying Social Security.
4. Schedule the viewing, service, burial, and care of your loved one.
5. Provide a limousine to transport the immediate family to the cemetery and back to the funeral home or church.
6. May provide a guest book for friends and family to sign.
7. Collect the cards that accompany the flowers and provide a box of thank you notes.

Tasks for You

1. Make personal calls to family and friends. Have this list prepared ahead of time.
2. Obituary –A draft can be done ahead of time and updated quickly. Read obituaries to get ideas.
3. Bring clothing, including underclothing, for your loved one. Don't forget eyeglasses.
4. Give a photo to the funeral home to show their hairstyle and makeup.
5. Ask friends or family to be ushers and pallbearers, then provide a list to your coordinator.
6. Prepare the order of service, including the list of who will speak, read the eulogy, quote scripture, pray, and perform music. The funeral home may provide the programs for you.
7. Video tribute or photo boards of your loved one's life. (Optional)

Last Minute Costs

1. Obituary costs are determined by the length of the newspaper article. They can range from $30 to $150 or more.
2. Weekend funerals may have an extra cost.
3. Spray of flowers for the top of the casket.
4. Food for the family and friends after the funeral.
5. Grave markers or headstones can be chosen later.

Rely on your coordinator, and delegate friends or family to complete some of the tasks.

A blessing for me was Clayton. For each parent, from hospice through the services, he stopped everything and took the lead. He wrote the obituaries and coordinated every detail with the funeral director. The plans had been made, and he executed them flawlessly. He facilitated the order of service, introducing each speaker, pastor, and family member. The caregiving had been my area, and fortunate for me, Clayton's strength was public speaking and the logistics of the funeral.

Fortunately, funeral homes are experts with the details, understand the importance of the occasion, and are experienced at walking the family through an emotional time.

Chapter 20

About the Sorrow
It's like no other pain.

The Truth Is...

How do you go from talking every day, putting on their pajamas, and eating every meal together to them being gone? They aren't in the next room taking a nap or sitting in the recliner talking to you right now. You can't pick up the phone and hear their voice. It's empty.

After Mom's funeral, the most difficult task was returning her Christmas presents. They were still under the tree. A pastel sweater, her favorite perfume, soft pajamas and a robe, a bright paisley scarf. Dad and I had felt such joy shopping and wrapping, but they had to be returned. I walked to the register at Macy's and blubbered the words, "My mom died. I'm returning her presents." The clerk had no idea what to do with me. I went to the fitting room and cried.

While caring for my dad, the sorrow was walking out of the care center and leaving him. It hurt. It wasn't every day, but many days were sorrowful. I missed him as his mind faded away. The fading away was sorrowful.

Still today, I drive by Lola's condo and remember honking as she waved goodbye to me. Don't tell anyone, but sometimes I honk the horn and say, "Hi, Lola."

The Impact of Close Caregiving

It took me a year before I recovered from Mom's last week. Her suffering, the ER, her pulling out the tubes, facilitating her final decision. The Lord gave me amazing strength for that time. But for the next year, I lived it over and over. I just couldn't shake it. So many spouses and children have shared this battle over a regret or a burden that won't let go. For most, it's a wish that they'd done something differently, second guessing themselves.

"If only I'd mentioned his stomach issue before it was too late."

"The level of nursing care for my wife was lacking."

"I should have been there so he wouldn't have fallen."

"Why didn't I figure out a way to care for her at home?"

"I regret yelling at my mom when I was frustrated with her."

"When Dad didn't answer the phone, I should have gone to check on him."

"Looking back now, I can see the symptoms."

"Did I let him go too soon?"

Keep Sorrow from Becoming Despair

Navigate through the sorrow by renewing your mind. Fill your thoughts with words that bring peace. Psalm 46:10

Be. (breathe)

Be still. (breathe)

Be still and know. (breathe)

"Be still and know that I am God."

Breathe. He's got this.

Sorrow Does Not Have a Plan

No stored happiness will diminish it.
No awareness of its nearness can soften the blow.
No muscle can push it away.
"Casting all your care upon Him, for He cares for you" (1 Peter 5:7).

Sorrow Drives You to Your Knees

About a month after my dad's funeral service, I had a good meltdown. As I sobbed, all I could say was, "I made it. I made it all the way through." I let myself feel the weight of the journey. It felt overwhelming as I looked back, but I had accomplished what God planned for me. I was not the same.

Sorrow Comes in Waves

A song, smell, a place, or a memory takes you off guard when you least expect it. Today or months away.

Back on December 22, 2013, I closed Mom's Bible and snapped the cover shut. The bookmark was still in place, and the lace of her hanky rested against the gold edge. My daughter had requested Grandma's Bible for a keepsake.

Four years later in 2017, our church was studying Nehemiah 2 as our Bible reading. That week I spent a few hours with my daughter and saw Mom's Bible on her shelf. It hadn't been opened since I closed it four years earlier. We sat with it for a minute, unsnapped the cover, and opened it.

"I wonder what she was reading her last day?"

As we moved the bookmark, Nehemiah 2:2 stared back at us. "Why is your face sad, since you are not sick? This is nothing but sorrow of heart." We both gasped. It brought us to tears remembering her and at the same time thinking, *What are the odds?* Nehemiah is probably one of the least read books in the Bible. Okay, Mom. It was just for us.

Sorrow Fades

Time is your friend. Life crowds back in. The first time you go back to a familiar spot, it can be sorrowful. But soon you will think of new things. You will think of your loved ones, but the sting will be replaced with loving memories. Time heals.

By now, you know my parents' favorite restaurant was Cracker Barrel. They dined there so often that everybody knew their name. The first time I went back, I could see them sitting at their favorite spot. I knew which items they would order, and their essence filled the room. It was sadness.

Now I smile at the thought of them and chuckle at remembering how we had to coax Mom to stop shopping.

Joy Stays

Through it all, God will give you grace, peace, and strength exactly when you need it, not a moment before.

"Weeping may endure for a night, but joy comes in the morning" (Psalm 30:5).

Chapter 21

I Wish I'd Known Then What I Know Now

Plan the Future, Live in the Present

"Your Word is a lamp to my feet and a light to my path" (Psalm 119:105).

God places a circle of light around your feet for today, then a guiding light for the path to come. Tasks for today that plan the future.

Today Illuminated: There's comfort in living in the present, one step at a time. What needs to be accomplished this day? Don't put off till tomorrow what has been revealed now.

The Future Illuminated: There's also confidence for the path ahead, life from God's perspective. Your future with your spouse, children, or parents as you follow God's will.

Starting with a Plan

I know. You don't want to even think about aging or planning for your own care. You want to skim over this section because you've lots of living to do. So let's put an exciting spin on it. Technology has made planning easy. You just must know two things—what to plan and when. In fact, the planning lessons in this book span three generations. If you're retired, you can be confident your plans are secured. If you're caring for parents, you'll see the ways to prepare for yourself. And if you're a young adult or young family, you can learn about caring and preparing.

This chapter also shows you what I wish my parents had planned. It would have changed everything because planning for care and learning to care go hand in hand. If you skip this step as a young family or senior adult, it will hamper your ability to care or be cared for. So right now, you have the unique opportunity to look at health and aging from several perspectives. As you read, you'll note the steps and the timeframe to plan for the unexpected.

In the Event of the Unexpected–Organize Now

The unexpected happens at every age—a sudden illness of a child or an accident as an adult that results in a disability or death. So how do you plan for the unexpected as a young spouse? Or when do you bring up the end-of-life topic to your aging parents? How soon should your young family get organized?

Common sense would say, "Now." But why? Because of the unexpected.

In Case I Die File

When our family was young, Clayton created a file called *In Case I Die*. It was written for the spouse or person left to manage the financial and personal details in case of an untimely death or if they are not capable of daily living skills.

Our file is simply a large manila envelope that includes lists and important documents and instructions. In January, we update the information and review what has changed. There's a cover page with a list of step-by-step instructions of what to do and who to call first and a table of the contents on the outside. It includes all contact information, passwords, and account numbers, along with financial accounts, list of assets, the funeral home, the attorney, the executor of the will, insurance policies, health records, our CPA, our pastor, and family contact numbers. It contains instruction about when and how bills are paid. Dave Ramsey's Legacy Drawer is a good online resource.

Amazon has planners you can purchase instead of a manila envelope. They list everything you need and provide pockets and pages for the information. Just search *in case I die*. *I'm Dead, Now What?* is one planner that I found, along with *Putting Things in Order*. My favorite is *Where I Buried the Bodies*. So have fun and find one that suits your personality.

Are there digital planners? Now we're talking. Everplans.com is a secure, encrypted, user-friendly planner. One-click and your designated person has instructions from you about health care, wills, insurances, documents, accounts, and contacts. This information and documents in a single file would be so important to me. Even though we both know the details, a step-by-step list would be a lifesaver in a trying time. However, when we update the information each year, we organize it detailed enough for our adult children.

What Plans Should Be Made Now?

Of course, there are countless documents for every scenario, but you only need the basics including a simple will, a one-page living will, and basic insurance. The advantages are priceless not only to you but your loved ones.

Wills: A will designates who receives your tangible assets and financial accounts. Anyone that owns something should have a will. It simplifies the process and provides clarity for your family when they need it most. Even more important, as parents of dependent children, you can name a guardian to ensure that the care of your children will be your decision. It can be a simple will completed online or with an attorney.

Living Will: A living will is your voice for your own care. A health document, a checklist of care options in case of severe injury or terminal illness when you cannot speak for yourself. It takes the gut-wrenching decision off the shoulders of a family member. You can choose options of care for your comfort and quality of life. The form can be downloaded by state and given to your primary care doctor, a family member, and in your file. Legalzoom.com and lawdepot.com have free online forms for living wills. Still another practical resource is ramseysolutions.com. The easiest form is from your physician.

We've all heard about patients with no hope of recovery kept alive by a machine. Some of these cases can go on for months and years. It divides and bankrupts families, but when your wishes are clearly documented and discussed ahead of time, it eliminates extra distress and conflict in your family.

Insurances: What would happen if you could never work again? A young man in his late twenties with a family was severely injured in a car accident. He had purchased disability insurance from his employer two years earlier and was relieved to continue receiving a large portion of his salary. This is unpleasant to consider. However, knowing that you have a monthly income if you become disabled is priceless security and quality of life for you and your family.

Along with the long-term disability insurance, a term life insurance policy, in case of death, will provide your family immediate finances. There are many quick resources such as Dave Ramsey's website that have clear options on the basic insurances that are vital to protect a young family.

How Can You Plan Financially Now for Later?

What's your retirement number? When we were in our thirties, Clayton and I discussed how much money we would need to retire. I wanted security, so I immediately said, "A house paid off." Clayton wanted a dollar amount. I wanted a roof. By combining those two goals, we planned based on our present salaries, which were pitiful at the time. But we began putting money aside monthly, took advantage of matching funds at work, and later began increasing savings from bonuses and raises.

Of course, we included family vacations in our budget, all while saving. But we lived below our means and put ourselves on a mission to become debt free. It meant smaller cars, saving for a twenty-percent down payment on a house, getting a fifteen-year mortgage, and a firm budget. Did it pay off? Yes. I have a debt-free roof over my head, and Clayton reached his number but kept working. That's another book. So what's your number? What's your plan?

Long-Term Health Insurance

How do you protect your retirement number? In our fifties, Clayton and I purchased long-term health insurance. This is the single most important money we spend for peace of mind and financial security. It covers nursing home or home care and protects our assets and savings. Even though our children don't realize it now, they'll thank us later. Boy, will they.

What prompted us to make this decision? We realized that most seniors require home, assisted, or nursing care. Without this long-term health insurance, retirees nervously make lifestyle adjustments and still worry if the money will last. This was the one insurance that we wished our parents had planned. It would have made a vast difference in their independence and access to care.

Even parents with financial resources want the confidence that assisted care or nursing is part of their retirement plan. When children have free access to caregivers, the finances become less complicated and easier to budget. The caregiving decisions are already made for them. The decision of whether to spend the money on your care is decided.

The long-term health insurance policy allows you the option of home care, assisted living, or a nursing care facility. Each policy has a variety of care levels and options so you can choose what you can afford in monthly premiums. The daily care allowance is adjusted up yearly for cost of care.

A long-term health care policy would have been priceless and utilized for all four of our parents. It would have made a tremendous difference in our ability to provide options for their care. Did I say tremendous difference? Oh my, yes. It would have provided their daily living care and preserved available assets and cash to pay their household bills.

Cognitive impairment, inability to bathe, dress, toilet, eat, transfer from chair to bed—depending on your policy, any two of these would trigger the policy to cover caregivers.

When Clayton's stepdad had his leg amputated, a long-term health insurance policy could have provided a caregiver for those ten years. Clayton's mom, Lola, also would have qualified for in-home care the final three years of her life. It would have paid for my father's care the last four years of his life and my mother at least the last six years.

So, if you are fifty-five to sixty years old, you can already be considering this policy as part of your retirement budget. These long-term health policies open the door for options that will take care of you and preserve your money. Yes, there is a monthly premium, but just imagine yourself as a senior and wanting to remain at home. Your children will be there, but the policy will provide the additional hands-on care or a facility if needed.

What to Plan Later

Should you make funeral arrangements now? What are the benefits of making your funeral arrangements early? The main benefit is that you are making your own choices, and more importantly, these arrangements aren't being made under duress, with emotions high, in a short timeframe, and with so much to do. No one is scrambling for how to pay for it or how much to spend or trying to decide what arrangements you would have wanted.

There are two simple reasons to make arrangements in early retirement: time and money.

Why Time?

After you retire, you begin formulating your plans and activities for the next part of your life. You start to get a sense of where you're going to live and what you're going to do. The time may be right to consider where you and your spouse will be buried. Maybe there is already a family plot somewhere, or perhaps this is the city where you plan to live with your family or near friends. Once you can narrow down the location and find a beautiful, well-maintained setting, there is plenty of time to plan and to pay.

Why Money?

My parents knew that they wanted to be buried in Jacksonville where they grew up, retired, and had family nearby. We learned that the prices for plots, caskets, and funeral expenses would continue to rise each year. So Dad priced the plots and did a repurchase through the paper of two plots together in a beautiful setting near a large tree. Then we made an appointment with the funeral home office and within an hour had picked out the caskets from a book and were given a list of all the associated costs. We didn't walk through rooms of caskets. We looked at pictures, pointed, and said yes. We walked out with a payment book, and Dad made monthly payments over five years. It was not depressing or morbid, just a thoughtful process completed in a business-like manner. However, afterward we did go to Dairy Queen for an ice cream comfort cone!

Around our sixty-year-old mark, Clayton and I followed our parents' example and made our arrangements. It's easier to do while you're working and have the resources and clarity of mind.

We made monthly payments for several years on our funeral arrangements. In September of 2021, we were informed that it was paid in full. So we called the kids to celebrate. Wouldn't you like to know how that call went? "Yay, we can die now." They were not amused, but we loved creeping them out just a little.

Basic Documents of Authorization

Bank Accounts: When your parents are in their late seventies or when their health begins to fail, begin adding your name to their accounts. My name was on my parents' checking account by the time they were seventy-five. My name was not printed on their checks, but I could write a check and pay bills. Now all you need is your name on their accounts, online access, and a debit card.

Power of Attorney: At some point, you will want a power of attorney. My parents and I went to an elder law attorney and wrote up a power of attorney that gave me authority to do any business for them. I used this power of attorney more than any other document. I made a digital copy also. Copies were sent to the financial institutions for proof of authority, which gave me permission to call on their behalf, ask questions and advice, and to access their money for their care until it was gone That's exactly what it was saved for, and I made sure that they received the attention they needed. Every penny. I had POAs on file for their health records, banks, bills, and accounts so I was allowed to open, close, and have access on their behalf.

Clayton and I did use our own money along the way, but I always kept money in Dad's account. Sometimes he would ask if he still had money in the bank, and I always said, "Of course you do." It was true, and he was satisfied.

Health Surrogate: This is a document giving me permission to make health care decisions for them if they can't make it for themselves. I used it. In fact, several of our older friends now have me as their health surrogate because they have no family nearby. Sobering thought, making life decisions for other people. Obviously, we are dear friends.

Conclusion—Not Inclusive

There are other financial and health safeguards to consider, but the ones listed are the essential documents that you will be relieved you accessed. Over time, at the right time, you can put each one carefully and simply into place. Decide which ones you can start now and put the others on a simple timeline. At least start having the conversations with your parents or with your adult children. Getting organized and sharing that information is a plan in itself.

Chapter 22

Are You Ready?

It's an absolute.

Are You Ready for Caring?

Love is a verb more than a noun. It's selfless to think more about someone else. This love is a state of mind, the way you carry yourself, and the character of how you face each day.

All the details of medicine, physicians, and hospitals will fade, but those precious moments will stay alive. Just like your living example will impact your family for generations, pleasing your Heavenly Father will last for eternity.

Are You Ready for Eternity?

You plan countless details of your life including friends, career, meals, education, and entertainment. Yet all this attention is given to plans that could be canceled or skipped. There is less thought about a place you will absolutely go, an event that cannot be canceled or skipped. Nothing is 100 percent sure except this absolute. Ten out of ten people die. You can't avoid it, and you alone must plan now where you will go at that instant. Years from now, tomorrow, or today.

Can you know what is beyond that thin veil between life and eternity? "You do not know what will happen tomorrow. For what is your life? It is even a vapor that appears for a little time and then vanishes away" (James 4:14).

"For God so loved the world that He gave his only begotten Son, that whoever believes in Him should not perish but have everlasting life" (John 3:16).

Your Heavenly Father wrote a book for you. "These things I have written to you who believe in the name of the Son of God, that you may know that you have eternal life" (1 John 5:13). Eternity is an absolute.

The book of John in the Bible is a starting place to plan for your eternity.

Don't miss Jesus.

About the Author

Photo credit: BY Amy www.armphoto4.com

Catherine Fitzhugh grew up in South Florida. She's a wife and mother with a long career as a schoolteacher and then administrator. Catherine stepped aside from her career to care for her parents. Her father had been caregiver to her mother during many years of illness, but when he was struck with a disease, the caregiver needed care. Because so many of her family and friends are standing at the threshold of caring, she was urged to write *Walk with Me.*

Made in the USA
Middletown, DE
06 April 2023

28360349R00095